SEEKING ADVERSITY

SEEKING ADVERSITY

HOW TO USE STRESS AND
EMBRACE LIFE'S DIFFICULTIES
TO REVEAL YOUR BEST SELF

CHRIS O'REILLY

NEW DEGREE PRESS
COPYRIGHT © 2021 CHRIS O'REILLY
All rights reserved.

SEEKING ADVERSITY
How to Use Stress and Embrace Life's Difficulties to Reveal Your Best Self

ISBN	978-1-63676-952-3	Paperback
	978-1-63730-018-3	Kindle Ebook
	978-1-63730-120-3	Ebook

This book is dedicated to my wife, Amanda. I love you.

Contents

	INTRODUCTION	11
CHAPTER 1.	SUFFERING	21
CHAPTER 2.	A VICTIM'S MENTALITY	37
CHAPTER 3.	WHY WE LOVE FICTIONAL CHARACTERS & WHAT WE CAN LEARN FROM THEM	55
CHAPTER 4.	FINDING A COMMUNITY	71
CHAPTER 5.	A SHOE ON THE WRONG FOOT	85
CHAPTER 6.	DELAYING GRATIFICATION	105
CHAPTER 7.	"MORE... TONED."	115
CHAPTER 8.	MOVEMENT & FINDING YOUR WHY	133
CHAPTER 9.	VULNERABILITY & HAPPINESS	145
CHAPTER 10.	SO DO IT.	157
	ACKNOWLEDGMENTS & FINAL THOUGHTS	173
	REFERENCES	179

"It is not the critic who counts; not the man who points out how the strong man stumbles, or where the doer of deeds could have done them better. The credit belongs to the man who is actually in the arena, whose face is marred by dust and sweat and blood; who strives valiantly; who errs, who comes short again and again, because there is no effort without error and shortcoming... and who at the worst, if he fails, at least fails while daring greatly, so that his place shall never be with those cold and timid souls who neither know victory nor defeat."

—THEODORE ROOSEVELT

Introduction

I stepped onto the scale. The familiar nurse checking me in at my primary care physician's office continued to slide the dial with a *clink-clink-clink* that caused a flinch with each grating noise indicating higher weight. It was the furthest right she had ever traveled on the old-fashioned scale. My weight: 285 pounds as a high school sophomore.

My doctor walked into the room after a short wait with my mom. I was already feeling self-conscious, but this was no different than the rest of the year. I had been too scared to call myself out for feeling uncomfortable with my obesity and not doing enough to fix this, largely because I lacked the emotional tools to cope with doing so. My doctor laid down the proverbial law with me. He addressed my weight first by asking if I was involved in any sports. I told him no. He double-checked because surely a high school junior isn't standing 6'3" and weighing in at 285 pounds *without* being a football offensive lineman. I assured him I was not involved—at least not anymore.

His demeanor grew grim. "Well," he began, "unless you do something about this, you can end up with all sorts of problems down the line." He explained that historically a young person who weighs this much only ends up putting on more weight as they grow older. More often than not, this leads to a litany of health problems, including heart issues, skyrocketing cholesterol, and even premature death. He then explained that, based on a few of my blood work results, I was already showing signs of these troubling trends.

After this talk, I was examined as part of a routine physical, but my mind was elsewhere. I was scared. I was ashamed. My mind and body seemingly shut down, and the fear of *what could be* overtook my whole existence. I was preoccupied by this fear in the months following even as I started down the path to bettering my health and losing weight.

During the drive home, I remember reading the visit summary as it sat temptingly on the center console of my family's car. My eyes traveled immediately to the top where my height and weight were filled in. According to my body mass index (BMI), I was sitting at a thirty-six: extremely obese.

That night, I sat in my room thinking about all the poor choices I had made. I ate too much of the wrong foods, I did not take exercising seriously, and I was a painfully shy student, so I often skipped out on social events. I allowed this cycle of shame and victimizing myself to run its course. Once my mind wanted out of this vicious cycle, I began to think rationally. Eventually, I discovered the one truth that would provide fuel for me to keep going: "Nobody is going to lose this weight for me. I'm in this circumstance right now. What can I do to change it?"

In the weeks that followed, I began running. It seemed like a sure, fast way to lose weight. My first day, I wanted to run a lap around my neighborhood's block, which was a full mile. I made it about two hundred yards before I stopped—my body screamed bloody murder from pain. And the pain did not discriminate it was everywhere. I walked home, my shins alternating between hot and cold soreness in the chilly November fall of suburban Chicagoland.

When I finally made it home, I felt utterly defeated. What I wanted to do—lose an enormous amount of weight—seemed horrifically long, arduous, and painful. If I was going to do this, I needed to suck it up like I never had before. Growing up comfortable, coddled, and actively avoiding stress had led me to this point, and with no coach, nutritionist, dietitian, physical therapist, or mentor in my corner, I would have to fend for myself.

Now this is not to say that my parents were not physically and emotionally present; I was fortunate to have both present throughout my life. They loved and supported me. When it came to this certain circumstance, I did not go out of my way to project outwardly that I needed help. In fact, very seldom did I speak of losing weight and turning my life around. This was on me. Later in my life, my tendency to internalize my fears and angst would rear its ugly head again. I would wade through the murky, sewer-like waters of severe depression and anxiety without a guiding light in the form of another person or group of people, including my parents.

Within two years of my visit to the doctor, and in a journey that I'll detail further within the book, I was down one hundred pounds. I became comfortable walking around when I was about eighty-five pounds down. As a senior in high school, I was voted a class representative in our high school's student government; I had discovered my voice. I began to introduce the concept of placing myself in adverse circumstances—often through workouts and runs—to fuel personal development and growth.

***

I found the story of David Goggins long after high school, at a time when I was in desperate need of internal growth. His life's tale is, on the surface, miraculous and seemingly superhuman. His accomplishments are numerous: he graduated both Navy SEAL training and Army Ranger School (as enlisted Honor Man in the latter), once held the record for most pull-ups done in twenty-four hours (over four thousand), and has run various ultramarathons (the distances of which typically exceed forty miles). He also qualified for what is considered the world's toughest race, the Badwater 135, by running in the San Diego One Day ultramarathon challenge where he completed one hundred miles running nineteen hours on broken feet with only a couple of days' notice to prepare.[1]

These accomplishments all sound like they were completed by Friedrich Nietzsche's Übermensch, Superman, or even Batman. And on many occasions and within interviews,

---

1 David Goggins, *Can't Hurt Me: Master Your Mind and Defy the Odds* (Austin, Texas: Lioncrest Publishing, 2018).

David has been told just that: he must be a superhuman living amongst ordinary people. His consistent answer, however, flips that script on its head.

According to David, he is no more inherently gifted or innately special than any other person in the world. What sets him apart is a simple concept, but it is one that is paradoxically viewed by most of the human populace. While most people avoid tense situations, Goggins often urges people to "stay in the fight." What does "stay in the fight" mean exactly?[2]

Life is not always fair, or easy, or even just hard. It can sometimes be downright painful, arduous, and can overcome people in subtle ways. Choosing to continue down a road that is comfortable—often leading to feeling merely adequate or mediocre—is one way life can exert this power. We don't always have to feel awful or burnt out to feel the full force of life. It can pound us into emotional numbness, and feeling just okay becomes the norm. We have "tapped out" of the fight with life.

Instead, according to David, what we should do to grow and achieve what we desire is run *toward* life's punches. Getting hit, taking it in, and *choosing* to respond is one of the most powerful things a person can do for themself. In this way, David actively seeks adversity and focuses on his weaknesses to fully round himself out as a human being. He teaches a metaphor related to the phenomenon of callousing: as our hands callous from repetitive use, so does our mind as we

---

2   Ibid.

continue to put it to work in adverse circumstances out of our comfort zones.³

David is a living, breathing example of one who harnesses the power of adversity to his advantage. Over the past year, I have spent a litany of time studying him and an array of others who have learned to harness the power of adverse circumstances and stressful situations, often by employing willpower and delaying gratification, to fuel personal growth and meaningful, positive change. These high achievers often have one trait in common: they view as an asset rather than a liability.

Stress is a ubiquitous term in the world today, and for good reason. Gallup's annual Global Emotions Report showed that most Americans (55 percent) reported feeling stressed a lot during the day in 2019. This represented the highest percentage of stress ever recorded for the US and was a full 20 percent above the world average of 35 percent. This stress correlates to negative experiences, and the increase of those experiencing negative experiences was the highest in over a decade, per Gallup.⁴

This stress is often the culprit for peoples' reasons for not continuing to pursue goals set for themselves. New fitness and dieting regimens often fall by the wayside when confronted with the short-sighted, fight-or-flight response triggered by the body's biological response to stress, according to Stanford health psychology professor and willpower guru Dr. Kelly McGonigal, PhD. The body's psoas muscle—the largest of the hip flexor group—is the "stress muscle." We physically

---

3   Ibid.
4   *2019 Global Emotions Report.* (Washington, DC: Gallup, Inc., 2019).

tighten this when under stress or duress, causing the body to begin to fold in on itself. As our mind begins to fold upon itself and call for retreat under extremely stressful conditions, so too does the human body.

David Goggins often mentions the one phrase that people confront him with: "I could *never* do what you did!" The prevailing worldview about challenging adversity and placing oneself amid a stressful situation is that people simply don't want to do it because of how Herculean it seems. It's a difficult ask, and in my experience, people tend to opt for the easier path. We as humans seek comfort and the path of least resistance to avoid feeling those negative emotions and the physically uncomfortable biological reactions associated with extreme stress. We don't want faster heartbeats, tighter hips, cold sweat, or flush on our faces; however, per Dr. McGonigal, stress gains this power by a deep-rooted belief by people that it is bad.

In a now-viral TED Talk called "How to Make Stress Your Friend" given in January 2013, Dr. McGonigal cites a study she evaluated at Stanford. She says that researchers found that people who answered yes to the question "Do you believe that stress is harmful for your health?" and experienced any level of stress were 43 percent more likely to die within an eight-year period than the other respondents. She stated that, according to the study's results, those who did not believe that stress was harmful for their health were the least likely to die during that eight-year span.[5]

---

5 TED. "How to Make Stress Your Friend | Kelly McGonigal." September 4, 2013, video, 14:28.

Believing stress is negative is simply human nature. It's what we are fed by societal consensus, and because of peoples' deep desire to be accepted and liked, we very often fall into the trap of believing what is on the surface of these consensus beliefs. One must deeply desire to believe something different and not care what others think about their beliefs. Personal accountability and deep, meaningful personal growth—these are concepts that a person must drive toward achieving by *wanting* them. Those who don't want to grow don't. Those who do might begin and find the first week to be invigorating; however, I am not interested in that first week. I *am* interested in hearing the story of how somebody who might be two years into their journey to bettering themself is faring. And what I can guarantee they will say is that they have faced hell and adversity.

This feeds precisely into what I believe. Instead of looking at adversity and stress as negative, they can and should be viewed as positive—or, at the very least, with little to no emotion. I lived long periods of my life not wanting to be challenged. The easy path was always the sought-after path. The moment I started feeling some anxiety, some soreness while working out, or some intellectual challenge in class that seemed entirely insurmountable, it was my nature to quit.

Today's most successful people do not live that way. The most successful individuals in our current society have learned to harness the power of adversity to become who they are truly meant to be. David Goggins, Spartan warriors, Octavia Spencer—these are but some of the people who have chosen to take the route of celebrating their failures as they do their successes and harnessing the power of stress within their lives.

I firmly believe that it does not take a special type of person to achieve greatness. What is wonderful about the concept of greatness is that it is entirely relative—so *you* get to strive to create your own idealization. Dr. Angela Duckworth, a psychology professor at the University of Pennsylvania and author of *Grit: The Power of Passion and Perseverance*, also went viral for a TED talk she gave about willpower and grit. In it, she outlines a study she conducted within a variety of settings, including the West Point Academy and public schools in rough neighborhoods, that had to do with predicting success for students. After a lengthy study, she and her research team concluded that one trait directly correlated to long-term success: grit.[6]

This study illustrates my point even further: for much of society, the qualities to push through adversity and use it productively are inherent within us. The idea that circumstances out of our control dictate that we cannot overcome and improve is patently false. However, the concept of pushing through adversity being easy and coming without any real effort or introspection is also wrong. Pushing on through a heavy emotional storm, while it requires a lot of effort dig one's hands into the proverbial landfill of our life's past challenges and adversity, can only lead to greater and more sustained success.

It is up to you—*and this might sound scary*. I know I was deeply scared. Sometimes fear still grips me. It can be overwhelming, and this mental state determines our physical

---

6   TED. "Grit: The Power of Passion and Perseverance | Angela Lee Duckworth," May 9, 2013, video, 6:12.

inaction and paralysis. My book is meant for those in college who are struggling to overcome peer pressure to "fit in"; those in high school who are struggling to figure out their personal identities while coming of age; and young adults who are wading through life's murky waters wondering, "What do I have to offer to the world?" Young professionals who feel stagnant in their work/life balance can also find great value out of my book. Finally, for those in their middle aged/senior years wondering how to find new purpose and joy in the seemingly mundane, my book is for you.

In short, if you are feeling stuck, pigeonholed, or misunderstood because of something unique about you or your personal situation in life, my book will hopefully help you understand the idea of facing down and overcoming your own personal adversity.

Throughout the book, I will share my journey through losing more than one hundred pounds twice in my life, lessons I have learned on the science of willpower and drive, and anecdotes and stories from some people whom I see as living and breathing *adversity seekers*.

CHAPTER 1

Suffering

I was late and sprinted with all the energy I could muster. It was February in Milwaukee during my senior year at Marquette University, and I had snow up to my knees with no signs of the blizzard ceasing. I stumbled my way through the snow en route to a rehearsal for *Frankie & Johnny in the Claire de Lune*—a favorite play of the Off-Broadway crowd—where I was to play Johnny. Trudging through a snowstorm is hard enough in good shape; however, I was over three hundred pounds with creaky knees, a suspect cardiovascular system, and a perpetually sore scalp.

Most would say that's a random spot to be sore, and I would agree. But you must have the fullest picture of me at my nadir. You need to understand the mode of desperation I was in—emotionally, physically, and even spiritually—that now, rather than pummeling me into submission, drives me.

The soreness on my scalp was due to literal sores, little open wounds that were perpetually open due to my nervous habit of picking at them. They would break, I would bleed and feel a brief wash of pain that felt oddly satisfying, snap myself back to the moment, and clean the wound. These stress sores, as I came to call them, began flourishing with regularity towards the conclusion of my junior year of college—nine months before my sprint through the torrential snowstorm. My body was showing me that it was stressed beyond the normal capacity for a human being. My creaky knees, a persistent dull ache in my right side, and a seemingly never-ending appetite also reminded me of my body's brokenness.

I regularly found culinary comfort in a large Domino's meat lover's pizza with a side order of Cinna Stix. Leftovers did not exist; I finished that entire meal in one sitting at least three times per week over the course of months. My exterior brokenness was mirrored by my interior, shattered in a million distinct pieces of emotional glass cutting my emotional being with even the slightest deviation from my tiny, phone booth-sized comfort zone. At the rate I was traveling, a more apt comparison could have been a coffin-sized emotional comfort zone.

I'm sure at this point you're wondering aloud, "Chris, you just talked to us about the weight struggle you had in high school. What happened?" That would be an insightful question. You're not reading this wrong. I didn't accidentally include this passage of being overweight and depressed here in Chapter 1. This was, in fact, the second time that I found myself struggling mightily with my weight and emotional health. After having lost weight in high school, I put it all back on in college and then some. The reality that I had failed myself by erasing the progress I had previously worked so hard to make also ate away at my core every day.

This is all to say that, as I trudged through the piercingly cold pellets of snow across campus to the small black box theater that my cast mate, director, and I were to rehearse in, I was not holding up very well. One of my regular respiratory viruses throughout junior and senior year popped up, so that was certainly not supplying me with extra energy. My obesity was making it difficult to function without a blanket of fatigue and multiple colds and sinus infections popping up regularly. I was at the peak of living unhealthily at the time, and while it took much less for my body to become ill, it took far more effort to heal.

The show was not one I was particularly excited about as the theater department had grown to be the albatross in my own life that hung around my neck due to its toxicity. As a non-theater, English major who regularly performed in shows with eager and competitive department personnel, there was certainly resentment towards me. There existed an inherent cliquey-ness to the group that could sometimes go above and beyond normal cliquey behavior. These people could be ruthlessly cold deceptively backstabbing.

On top of this attraction to drama, these few theater majors were resentful when I was cast as the lead in two main stage shows in the same year. Sarcasm, passive aggression, and—by the time I was a senior—excessive time in that toxic environment took a heavy toll on me. I was going to a place that no longer brought me comfort; instead, the theater brought on feelings of anxiety and fear that permeated my every thought. I stayed hoping that I would re-discover this love and comfort. At its best, performing on stage triggered a dopamine release that helped me feel as if I was not only having fun but was also helping others to do the same. At its worst, performance became an escape from everyday life because it afforded me the opportunity to play a character and live the life of somebody else. By my senior year, I was actively looking forward to living anybody's life but my own.

***

For some specific context, I happened upon Marquette's theater department through my foray into improv. comedy with the campus improv. group. After making the group, I decided that, rather than another international politics course, I should try something more to do with my newly discovered artistic outlet of performing and writing. There was an open spot in a playwriting course for the spring semester and I jumped.

During the course, we would perform short, improvised scenes to inspire material to write. The professor, the then de facto head of the theater department, took notice. She was to direct the upcoming fall production of *The Foreigner*, a comedy that originated in Milwaukee, for Marquette's main stage season. Auditions would be held in the coming week. She personally gave me a script following class one day and told me to specifically hone in on Charlie. I had no idea how big or small a role of Charlie was; based on my limited experience in theater, I assumed it was a bit part.

Boy was I wrong. Charlie was the *lead* of the show. The more I read, the more I saw CHARLIE in the unmistakable Samuel French script-style font. I became both enamored with and nervous about the prospect of being a lead in any show, not just one that would play on the Marquette main stage. That was where Chris Farley, the performer whom I grew up idolizing, had performed so regularly. Potentially performing in the same space was an overwhelmingly exciting idea.

***

As I closed in on the building, I stopped to catch my breath. I paused my iPod and glanced around. The sky was grey and blurry with sheets of snow and streetlamps providing orbs of light in the darkness. I looked up at the dilapidated dorm building that housed the theater and caught a glimpse of myself in the door's glass front-turned-mirror. I remember thinking out loud, "Is this really it? Is this who I am, and who I'm supposed to be?" At that rehearsal, there was plenty of sarcasm to go around about my sickness and how under the weather I *really* was. On the surface, they were right. It was a virus, but nothing I hadn't dealt with before. It was unsettling, however, to know that my more severe illness wasn't overtly visible, and it did not help that I was a self-certified expert in hiding that illness from others.

Rehearsal came and went in three and a half hours. It was 9:30 p.m. as I began my twenty-minute walk back home across campus in a snowy but settled downtown Milwaukee before my 8:00 a.m. class the next morning. As I left, I searched for "The Rock" on Google—I am still not completely sure what came over me here. After sifting through images of geographic marvels of hardened sediment and stills of Sean Connery from the eponymous movie, I found who I was looking for. Dwayne Johnson, the former WWE Heavyweight Champion and then-burgeoning actor had proven an inspiration to me because of a credo he regularly shared on social media: "Always be the hardest worker in the room." Through following him on Facebook, Twitter, and Instagram, one could see that he *lived it.*

I walked home listening to various interviews of his on YouTube. There was one through line that permeated—his "anchor" that kept his two feet on the ground was getting up early and working out. He had a principle that *no matter what,* he would do it. I began to tell myself that if The Rock could go from having seven dollars in his pocket and wrestling at flea markets to fame and great success, I could at least make it to the gym the next day. I opened a blog that I kept at the time and wrote all about how I needed to put myself on a diet, make it to the gym, and hold myself accountable to myself and others. I was sick and tired (very literally at that moment), but mostly I was sick and tired of *being* sick and tired.

I went to Marquette's rec center the next day. I was cumulatively more uncomfortable than I had been in the three years prior all put together. Three twenty-pound kettlebell swings were a struggle with those creaky knees. A treadmill might as well have been an instrument specifically invented to torture my entire body. Attempting to decipher the resistance and weight machines' picture-based instructions was like reading a foreign language. After about twenty minutes, I threw in the proverbial towel and walked my way home. I didn't even take the time to put my sweatpants back on and walked home in the ten degree weather without any leg or torso warmth. But I didn't feel it. I was upset, and looking back now, I realize why.

Self-control transformed into a term that meant nothing to me. I was not familiar with willing myself through any difficult circumstances. I did not use my experience to help raise my confidence and grow bold in the face of adversity. Instead, when confronted with difficult circumstances, I shrunk physically and emotionally, and I often panicked. I sought comfort everywhere—in food, in avoiding school to sleep in my apartment, and even by shirking responsibilities in my relationships with friends. I became a recluse, and years had passed by before I realized it. The years when people are supposed to grow into adults and transition into adulthood promptly moved right by me as my eyes were seemingly closed. I so desperately wanted to feel in control again. And that became what drove me.

***

The concept of suffering leading to growth has a rich history. It's an idea that finds some of its earliest origins in ancient Greece with the Spartan society instilling this discipline into every citizen: man, woman, and child. This was rare for the time because women were still regarded as second class citizens throughout most of the rest of the world, but the goddess Athena was the patron and face of justice and strength. Spartan women were proud, strong, and held voices at the highest level of government. Gorgo, Queen of Sparta and the wife of the renowned King Leonidas I, was once asked why a Spartan woman could govern men. She replied, undeterred: "Because we are the only ones who give birth to real men."[7]

---

[7] Hugh Liebert, *Plutarch's Politics: Between City and Empire* (New York: Cambridge University Press, 2016), 120-121.

Those Spartan men often governed by women were subject to a life full of prescribed adversity and suffering through the long and arduous agōgē physical training and educational program.[8]

Spartan males began their training quite literally at birth. Elder Spartans, present at the birth of a given male, would bathe the baby boy in wine because the Spartans held the belief that this ritual would prove to show the baby's mettle. Following a full body inspection, the baby would either be determined fit or unfit; if unfit, the child would be placed at the base of Mount Taygetus for another round of testing.[9]

This test was anything but superfluous; at its core, this was a given to the Spartan people directly from God. It was deeply embedded within the people of Ancient Sparta's psyches. It was so important that, should the elder Spartan council return days later to find the child alive, he would be proven worthy. Otherwise, most infants died of exposure. This horrific act illustrates the awful lengths that the Spartans would go in the quest to adhere to the mythos of suffering.[10]

This practice even inspired the legend of Romulus and Remus. Throughout each translation of the myth, the through line mostly remains as such: the twin brothers were left on the bank of the river Tiber by their mother Rhea Silvia following a decree by the king that they should die for representing a

---

8 "8 Reasons It Wasn't Easy Being a Spartan," History Channel Online, Evan Andrews, accessed January 3, 2020.
9 Ibid.
10 Ibid.

threat to his rule. Tiberinus, the patron of the river, intervened to save them from death and shepherded them along to various animals—including a she-wolf—for raising until their discovery by a local farmer. Romulus would later infamously and allegedly kill his brother en route to founding the city of Rome.[11]

At age seven, the boys enrolled in the Spartan agōgē, which would prove to be a thirteen-year quest essential to the growth of each Spartan male. Spartan culture held the dogmatic belief that a successful life would undoubtedly lead to an equally if not more successful afterlife, where praise and adulation would find them again. Each citizen, while surely fearful of certain situations at their very core, found great honor in dying for this very reason. It is only through this lens that one can begin to understand why Spartans acted so severely and often so barbarically.[12]

Throughout the arduous agōgē, each boy and young man was educated on Spartan culture, politics, society, how to be a properly contributing citizen, and the Spartan military history and strategy. By age twelve, boys were given only one article of clothing and underfed purposefully to teach them to steal and scrounge for food on their own. If caught, they faced harsh lashings. Already, this innate encouragement of adversity was training their minds to adjust to the sensation of hunger so that it would not be an issue during battle.[13]

---

[11] Ibid.
[12] Ibid.
[13] Ibid.

At every turn during a young Spartan man's journey, competition and ruthlessness was pushed to harden their minds, encourage unbeatable resiliency, and continue the tradition of possessing the world's then-foremost fighting force. The Spartan culture as a whole embraced the idea of adversity to fuel growth or quite literally die in the process.

The Spartan belief in adversity fueling growth has taken on its own life even in modern culture. The 2007 action film *300*, based on the now-legendary tale of the stand of three hundred Spartan soldiers against the Persian army of ten thousand plus, became the tenth highest grossing movie of 2007. The film, based on the graphic novel series of the same name and historical battle of Thermopylae, showcased the hardened Spartan way of life through stylish storytelling, Queen Gorgo's strong presence, and pithy dialogue, including the now famous "This is Sparta!" catchphrase for internet lovers everywhere.[14]

As the 2010s began, so too did the now popular Spartan Race phenomenon. Founded officially in 2007 by Joe De Sena, the obstacle-based races became popular in part for incorporating the ethos of ancient Sparta into the company's mission and vision. De Sena seeks to encourage, "that natural, human instinct that emerges when we put down our smartphones and go for a run in the woods. *In moments of adversity*, it kicks into action and gives us strength." This is a quote taken directly from Spartan Race's website.[15]

---

14 *300*, directed by Zach Snyder (2007; Burbank, CA: Warner Bros. Pictures, 2013), Blu-ray Disc.

15 "What is Spartan?," The Origin of Spartan, Spartan Race, accessed January 5, 2019.

By basing his company's ethos on that of ancient Sparta's warrior culture of adversity seeking, De Sena continues to see growth. There now exists the Spartan Races World Championships, an annual event begun in 2017 that attracts top tier athletic talent. It is sponsored by Reebok as of this book's writing.[16]

This is all to say that, in Spartan culture, to suffer for growth was not a question; rather, it was a mandate put forth to every citizen to fulfill duty to the city-state. While they undoubtedly took it to the extreme, this lifestyle of active adversity seeking and immersion still resonates loudly to this day. It resonates both due to and despite an evolving culture that encourages quick fixes and easier, more automated outcomes.

The meaning of the Greek word *pathos* is suffering/emotion, and the Ancient Greeks believed suffering to be the root of knowledge and knowing oneself. The actual etymology of "suffering" derives from the prefix "sub," meaning below or under, and "ferre", meaning "to endure/bear."[17] The Greek philosopher Aeschylus, in his famous play *Agamemnon* writes, "wisdom is the child of pain."[18]

As society evolved beyond the ancient Greeks, the attitude towards voluntary and necessary adversity and suffering seeking remained. With the rise of modern religion, especially during the medieval period, citizens of the world more frequently put themselves through arduous trials

---

16 Ibid.
17 *The Ooda: The Lifestyle of Awareness* (blog), *Medium*, January 1, 2014.
18 *Agamemnon*, trans. Robin Bond (Christchurch, New Zealand: University of Canterbury, 2014), line 177.

through a variety of means, including fasting. This was often done as means of purification, atonement, or simply self-betterment to contribute more meaningfully as a member of society. Per famed medieval historian Giles Constable in his 1982 piece *Attitudes Toward Self-Inflicted Suffering in the Middle Ages*, however, the citizens of the Middle Ages did not necessarily enjoy this. In theory, he posits, "The sufferings of the saints, and the stories of their lives, may have played something of the same role (of inspiration) in medieval society."[19]

In 1906, famed Austrian philosopher Rudolf Steiner wrote and presented an entire lecture on the context of suffering and its understanding by humans throughout time. Part of a larger series on the origins of evil, illness, and death, it was aptly called "Origin of Suffering." In it, he goes to great lengths to explain that, throughout the course of time, man has worried greatly about suffering because it "appears as a destroyer of peace, as a damper-down on the pleasure and hope of life."[20] He quotes famed philosopher Friedrich Nietzsche to further illustrate this point. Nietzsche said, "The best of all things is something entirely outside your grasp: not to be born, not to be, to be nothing. But the second-best thing for you is to die soon." Steiner uses Nietzsche's argument of the tragedy of birth to assert that suffering plays a deeply significant role in a person's life.[21]

---

19 *Attitudes Toward Self-inflicted Suffering in the Middle Ages* (Brookline, Mass: Hellenic College Press, 1982), 21.
20 Rudolf Steiner, "The Origin of Suffering," lecture, Berlin, November 8, 1906, transcript, The Rudolf Steiner Internet Archive and e.Lib.
21 Friedrich Nietzsche, *The Birth of Tragedy*, trans. William A. Haussmann (Boston: Digireads.com Publishing, 2018), 34.

Suffering's significant role is not, however, the stereotypically negative one, Steiner argues. By illustrating the journeys of the poetic tragic hero and Jesus Christ, where there is great suffering and challenge before an illustrious end of triumph and victory over death, he asserts that "it must indeed seem to us as if in some way suffering is connected to the highest in man."[22]

Nietzsche remains not only one of the world's most famous philosophers but also one of the most oft-cited secular philosophers who believed in the need for struggle to live a fulfilling life. As a proclaimer that "God is dead," he felt that the need for suffering came not as a mandate from a higher spiritual power; rather, he believed that it existed in part as a means to discovering one's purpose on earth. Gone were any notions connecting suffering to God's plan, which stands in direct contrast to the beliefs of the Spartans or the Middle Ages.[23]

Nietzsche extolled the virtue of hardship and suffering in his 1882 book *The Gay Science*, which was the same work in which he proclaimed "God is dead." He writes,

"Ask yourselves whether a tree which is to grow proudly heavenward can dispense with bad weather and tempests: whether disfavour and opposition from without, whether every kind of hatred, jealousy, stubbornness, distrust, severity, greed, and violence do not belong to the favouring circumstances without which a great growth even in virtue is hardly possible? The

---
22   Steiner, "Suffering," The Rudolf Steiner Internet Archive and e.Lib.
23   *The Gay Science*, trans. Thomas Common (Edinburgh: The Darien Press, 1910), 56-57.

poison by which the weaker nature is destroyed is strengthening to the strong individual—and he does not call it poison."

***

Each point in my journey has proven that suffering and adversity do possess a deep connection to the best within people. As I suffered physically through working out for the first year, spiritually through a deep doubt in God, and emotionally with clinical depression and anxiety albatrosses, I also grew. I became a force of momentum through the muddied times of negativity. Now, when I am met with a circumstance that is adverse and deeply challenging, I have learned to take a deep breath, smile, and proceed how I feel is best for *me*.

Now, this is not at all to say that I don't have days that feel heavier and harder than usual. Unfortunately, for those readers who are living with depression, anxiety, or any mental illness, these are powerful forces that need to be accounted for on top of all the other responsibilities life deals. The true ebbs and flows of living with a mental illness cannot go unacknowledged; I would be completely disingenuous if I didn't say that I struggle plenty even now.

If you do feel your problem is related to mental illness, there is only one option: seek the help and care of a medical professional. It has turned my life around—I now take two pills (an anti-depressant and an anti-anxiety med) every day to keep my brain chemistry near balanced.

After a lifetime of living with anxiety and depression, however, bad habits—some formed as a child—became part of the fabric of me. As an adult, I have still dealt with the ripple effect of these habits having been formed during such an impressionable time. Oftentimes, I do not want to go train. I have never liked running. I am naturally a "sit in front of the TV for a movie marathon" type of person. Putting myself through a physical ringer seven days a week does not sound "fun" to me some days, but that is precisely the point: suffering means placing yourself in those situations even when you *don't* want to or "feel" like it. It's on those days that you grow more than any other—by deciding to do whatever it is you may be procrastinating or putting off, you choose to expand your mind and personal horizons.

When you give yourself no way out and instead say, "I am not leaving until I'm finished," you begin to tackle the task at hand for truly what it is. You leave yourself no option to quit. So, instead, you need answers and solutions on how to get through. To do this, you must look inward—only when you begin to know yourself can you start to discover and celebrate your innate capabilities and powers.

> *Suffering and adversity taught me to look inward for answers.*

For some, this may seem too ambitious of an ask—to take a detailed personal inventory on your emotional, spiritual, and physical life can seem painful.

It is much easier to look askance in the mirror instead of gazing directly into your own eyes. Holding eye contact is a powerfully confrontational demeanor, and sometimes it takes confronting yourself to stop letting yourself off the hook.

You get to play the role of your best friend here. I define best friend as somebody who will tell you what you *need* to hear and not what you *want* to hear in times when we might be struggling. I once had a professor say, "We would never talk to others as we talk to ourselves." So, if a best friend were to sit down with you to let you know about concerning behavior they have observed, I know one thing is for certain. I would be inclined to listen.

CHAPTER 2

A Victim's Mentality

I bookmarked a video in 2017 of a young, recently retired Navy SEAL giving an impassioned speech. He described in vivid detail his upbringing with an abusive father. With a chillingly matter-of-fact tone, he recounted a painful memory of his father dragging his mother down the stairs by her hair in his childhood home. He reacted at first how you might expect a child to, with utter shock and horror. After these sensations washed over, instinct took the wheel, according to him. He sprinted down the stairs, jumped on his father's back, and began punching as hard as his five year old self could muster. His father shoved his mother to the side and turned his attention to David. These beatings, often executed in the same way, would remain a constant throughout his childhood and teenage years.[24]

He shared more trials of his life, including those that happened during his Navy SEAL training and its infamous Hell Week of one hundred and twenty hours of continuous

---

24 *Goalcast*, "How to Conquer Your Mind and Embrace the Suck | David Goggins," November 11, 2017, video, 10:31.

physical training with four hours of sleep randomly mixed in. Most people go through that process once, with most not making it through. Due to injury, he experienced three Hell Weeks in the span of a year.[25] It was during this time that he met the late SEAL officer Michael Murphy and Marcus Luttrell: two SEALs immortalized in the latter's powerful tell-all book *Lone Survivor*.

David would go on to raise more than $1 million for the Special Operations Warrior Foundation, a non-profit whose money goes towards benefiting the children of fallen special operators.[26] In 2005, he began to undertake this by running the San Diego One Day ultramarathon: a twenty-four hour race to see how many times one could run around a one mile track. He did 101 in seventeen hours without having trained at all. He would later become the pull-up record holder for most done in a twenty-hour period with 4,030 pull-ups as the new record. He also finished in the top five at a series of ultramarathons (those that are fifty miles or longer). He spoke from brutally painful experience, and his passion came from nobody and nowhere other than inside of himself.[27]

Goalcast, the popular inspirational social media presence, published this video. I would often open it up when I needed to feel and to hear how a driven person speaks. I decided to Google the man in the video by the name given in the title, David Goggins. This simple search changed my life.

---

25 Ibid.
26 "Mission, Vision and Values," Who We Are, Special Operations Warrior Foundation, accessed January 11, 2020.
27 *Goalcast*, "How to Conquer Your Mind and Embrace the Suck | David Goggins," November 11, 2017, video, 10:31.

Goggins speaks only from his personal experiences—which is more than enough. His past life forms his future decisions. He preaches that suffering is essential to personal growth. According to David, to discover and effectively measure your grit and willpower, you must actively place yourself in situations that are uncomfortable and stressful. It is during these times, he says, that people learn to think through their current situation rather than giving in to the fight or flight instinct.[28]

As I read David Goggins' book and watched his interviews, what I was struck with most is how he speaks candidly about his flaws and perceived shortcomings. He owns that, following an unsuccessful attempt at becoming an Air Force special operator, he returned to his adopted small hometown in Indiana and sprayed for cockroaches on Ecolab's staff. He weighed nearly three hundred pounds and was depressed. It was during this time that he found himself in what he calls "the victim's mentality."[29]

Much of his background and story resonated heavily with me. I began to devour every podcast and TV interview of his. I was uncomfortable, however, with one portion of his message: the victim's mentality. I couldn't be struggling with this, could I? I would later find that by asking that question, I was already answering it with an affirmative.

When a person feels stuck in limbo and is sinking in a slow tedious cycle of the quicksand of life, it is much easier to feel

---

28   Ibid.
29   Ibid.

sorry for oneself. You might think, "This could happen to nobody but me." Feeling sorry for yourself is a powerful trick the mind often plays because of how routinely successful it is. On the surface, the harder choice when faced with adversity is to retain a positive attitude. "Look on the bright side," your sunny friend might advise you, "it could always be worse!" It could most of the time, but this is a temporary bandage that cannot heal our deeper wounds.

In the cases of me and David Goggins, we were both overweight, despondent, and actively avoiding what made us uncomfortable. He struggled with a learning disability.15 I struggled with severe depression and anxiety. Our willpower muscles were falling out of shape. Like any other muscle group, to strengthen your willpower and grit, you *must* put yourself in situations that are uncomfortable and work it out. Otherwise the victim's mentality is ready and waiting to take you into its "comfort" and assure you that "you deserve to miss a workout today" or "homework can wait until tomorrow." While there are absolutely moments where breaks are necessary to recharge and restore mental and physical energy, these cannot become a crutch. Too many breaks mean the potential to slip into complacency, and the urge to remain at rest. Isaac Newton's first law of motion says that an object at rest tends to stay at rest, while an object in motion tends to stay in motion at the same speed unless acted upon by an unbalanced force.[30]

An unbalanced force can most definitely be fatigue, injury, or burnout for a human being. In that case, the unbalanced

---

30 "Newton's Laws of Motion," Science, Brittanica, accessed January 12, 2020.

force will call for a meaningful rest. Life won't relent, however, and neither should you. Once you have begun to see progress in each area of your life, gauging when and how to take a break in a way most effective for *you* will become clearer. Only when we really know ourselves and our personal sensibilities and needs can we restore ourselves.

According to David, human beings are often stuck with a governor on their internal 'engines.' For those who are not auto savvy—like I sure am not—a car governor keeps the speed on a car set at a particular pace.[31] So if the governor is on for the car at ninety miles per hour, the car will not exceed ninety and will begin to slow down once it reaches that speed. It is this mental governor, David says, that people need to get rid of to continue past any perceived limits.[32]

That is not done overnight. It takes constant practice, which often means putting yourself in those uncomfortable situations. Personally, as I began to lose weight and turn around my unhealthy eating and drinking habits, I would of course *always* want to quit almost immediately when I began my workout. Running at close to three hundred pounds was hellish. I had shin splints, tendonitis in both knees, and a bloated gut perpetually from not hydrating and eating properly. My clothes did not fit right. I tried to squeeze into smaller clothes too soon, and rather than swallow my superficial pride and change into more comfortably fitting outfits, I often kept these ill-fitting ones on. That bloated gut then began hanging over jeans that were a size or two too small, and I was

---

31 *Merriam-Webster*, s.v. "governor (n.)," accessed January 2, 2020.
32 David Goggins, *Can't Hurt Me: Master Your Mind and Defy the Odds* (Austin, Texas: Lioncrest Publishing, 2018), 210.

perpetually uncomfortable. I used to question whether there would ever come a day that I could genuinely fit comfortably into those jeans, and on a deeper level, ever regain a semblance of any self-confidence.

***

Any semblance of a positive self-image was eradicated during my college career. My victim's mentality and mental governor were enhanced due to the depression and anxiety that I'd developed over the course of my college career, but I would make sure to win every day with a workout that made me sweat, which did not take much at first. My diet came along parallel to this. Because feeling bad for myself had gotten me to that point, it took looking at myself over and over again and re-committing to changing my lifestyle over and over again.

This constant pounding takes not only grit and willpower but also an immense amount of patience and trust in yourself. Admittedly, patience, trust, grit, and willpower are all elements that I am not a natural at employing.

The first time I actively employed my own cookie jar was the spring of 2019. I was participating in the Memorial Day Murph CrossFit challenge. Within the CrossFit community, there are designated "workouts of the day," with some being named after fallen service members. The Murph was named after the aforementioned Navy SEAL Lieutenant Michael P. Murphy who, upon being surrounded on a mountain in Afghanistan, was killed while calling for back-up on an exposed ridge line. He actively put his life at risk to do so, and as he was shot, his final words uttered to SEAL support were, "Roger that, sir. Thank you."[33] He was awarded the Medal of Honor posthumously and was later depicted by the actor Taylor Kitsch in the 2013 film *Lone Survivor*.

Every Memorial Day, the CrossFit community does the Murph to honor his life and all those who have fallen in the line of duty. Growing up with two grandfathers who served in the European theater of World War II, I was instilled with a deep gratitude and appreciation for the military.

I chose to undertake the Murph Challenge first in 2018. The challenge itself consists of a one-mile run, followed by one hundred pull-ups, two hundred push-ups, and three hundred body weight squats—done in any order and to be broken up however is best for each person—before ending with one final mile run. It was by far the hardest task, mentally and physically, that I had ever undertaken. My aim was in part to honor the service members, like Mike Murphy, who had so selflessly given their lives in the name of protecting our freedoms here in the US.

I decided I wanted to do this in the fall of 2017. I was living at home and regularly commuting to downtown Chicago to visit my then-girlfriend, now-wife. I was also enrolled in The Second City's conservatory program, which is akin to a graduate school for improv. and sketch comedy. It's the theater where Steve Carell, Chris Farley, Tina Fey, and Stephen Colbert—amongst a many others—cut their comedy teeth. A

---

33 Steve Balestrieri, "Remembering Navy SEAL Michael P. Murphy, Medal of Honor 6/28/2005," *SOFREP*, June 29, 2017.

six-level program, I was enrolled in the Sunday class. Every weekend, I would stay downtown with my girlfriend, go to class on Sundays, have dinner with her after, and finally drive home late Sunday night.

Normally Sundays were reserved for getting in the right headspace and physical shape to perform for three hours in class, but one of these Sundays was different. As I made my way to class, I was confronted with an unusually dense crowd—it was friends and family of those participating in that fall's Chicago marathon. This hit me in a very particular place and in a life-altering way.

We all have our moments of doubt, questioning, and uncertainty—it's part of being human to feel that way. In this moment, as I saw a few athletes run by with friends and family actively cheering them on, I realized that my physical training could go up several levels higher than where it currently was. Seeing those runners give absolutely every ounce that their bodies, minds, and souls could give caused a rush of passion, doubt, and drive to run through me all at once.

That year of living at home saw me working out and training unconventionally. I was not in a financial place to belong to any gym nor was I in a mental headspace to carve out time to drive there and back before undoubtedly commuting downtown to Chicago during rush hour several times a week. Instead, I ran around my family's neighborhood for about ten to fifteen minutes before making it home to do light weightlifting. I do mean this literally: I had a singular dumbbell that weighed around twenty-seven pounds. I had a high resistance band with handles to do more resistance training, but that was the extent of my weightlifting equipment. To supplement, I would do calisthenics every once in a while—but I was, again, not mentally strong enough to bring myself to truly push past my mental, physical, and spiritual limits. Push-ups and bodyweight squats were where my calisthenics began and ended.

Seeing the marathon runners plug away somehow caused this realization to punch me in my soul's gut. I had difficulty focusing in class. All I could think about instead was, "What am I going to do to fix this uncomfortably comfortable place I'm in and forge ahead?" I scoured my brain for what I could do. Marathon training, while it provided an answer to this question, was counter to what I sought at the time—I was more interested in the CrossFit community and the focus on calisthenics with cardio exercise and weightlifting. This was when a social media video published by the actor Chris Pratt on Memorial Day 2017 came sprinting to the forefront of my mind.

Chris Pratt was another person whom I admired. Along with being a seemingly genuinely kind man devoted to his family, he also was dedicated to staying in top shape for his career, to which he was also devoted. For an aspiring comedic performer, he seemed to be "my type." He underwent a very public transformation that saw him lose a great amount of body fat, and now that he was in shape, he was putting his change to good use. He spent a portion of his 2017 Memorial Day doing the Murph Challenge, and this was when I first heard about the workout. When I learned what it entailed, I immediately wrote it off. Only in my *dreams* could I do that. Even then, I bargained, that seemed like a fifty-fifty proposition. For a long time, I was right—it took seeing those marathon runners to change that mindset.

I was inspired and disgusted all at once on Chicago Marathon Sunday in 2017—inspired seeing marathon runners chase greatness and disgusted by my own mindset. I vowed that I would do the Murph Challenge that following Memorial Day 2018. And doing that meant confronting a whole list of personal insecurities, one of which was that I was deathly afraid of pull-ups.

***

As an overweight kid trying to maintain some dignity in the eyes of his classmates, the Presidential Physical Fitness Test was the very bane of my existence in grade school. Most who have gone through elementary, junior high school, and high school in the US have done this; in case you haven't, the Presidential Physical Fitness Test was a physical ringer of tests comprised of various events. A rope climb, pull-ups, sit-ups, a mile run, and sit-and-reach all tormented me. And it happened for eleven straight years, ages six to seventeen. With every year that passed, my dread only heightened.

The pull-ups were a special kind of torture for me. It represented the most humiliating of the tests in elementary school as the kids who possessed no natural upper body strength or were overweight were left to a singled-out embarrassment in front of their class. In my experience, we (the gaggle of kids who could never get a single pull-up) were forced up to the pull-up bar, which was barely blue any more from the rust and chipped paint from what looked like 1968. One at a time, we were then forced to "jump" up and grab the bar with either an over or underhand grip. In a final tormenting move, the child who could not clear their chin above the bar by pulling up was forced to dangle for a good ten to fifteen seconds. There were a few token flexes and grunts as if there was any effort going into the sad affair of dangling, and the gym teacher would then call the child down and the next classmate to step up.

This was as public a humiliation as there ever was for me and plenty others in grade school. I looked at the boys who could do them with awe and confusion: they could do a whole number of pull-ups, but how? Because my Catholic elementary and junior high school was not overly large, we had the same physical education teachers throughout first through eighth grade. So they had a refined idea of who could probably do pull-ups, who might surprise them that particular year, and which kids were still stuck. Still, everybody was called as if there was a chance because everybody needed to participate.

Now, looking back, this was another experience that left a lasting impact on me. I actively avoided doing pull-ups until the fall of 2017. Only once did I ever venture over to a pull-up bar to even try: it was in Marquette's weight room. I tried, failed to lift any more than I had as a grade schooler, and was made fun of by a rugby player in the process for failing. Since that one moment six years prior, I had not even dared to look at a bar. But that had to change now that I decided to do the Murph. I had six months to not only learn to do pull-ups, but eventually bring myself to do one hundred in a timely manner.

After returning home from my impactful Sunday at the Chicago Marathon, I did my usual workout the following day. I began with a run around the block, and before I walked inside to "lift," I stopped and noticed the tree in our front yard. It had a thick branch that protruded from its middle that sat at what seemed from afar about pull-up bar height. I sauntered over, timidly, to more carefully inspect. Hoping I was wrong, I immediately broke into a sweat when I recognized I was right: it was the perfect height, and after dangling briefly, it held my weight comfortably. My experiences in gym class, those in Marquette's weight room, and all the moments I fell on my face while en route to losing weight all rushed to my mind. I began to psyche myself out when I surprised myself. I jumped up almost without thinking. I did one pull-up. I lowered myself. I did a second. After lowering myself two more times, I did four.

Following my fourth, I practically leapt away from the branch. More surprised and shocked than excited, I seemingly wanted to know how that just happened.

Before I went inside, I did six more; in my first ever "pull-up session," I did ten. More focused than ever, I decided to count that as my first day of training. I had done pull-ups—two of the components necessary to a successful Murph. Over the course of the next six months, I moved in with my girlfriend to a beautiful condominium complex in downtown Chicago that came complete with a gym on the top floor. I dove into the equipment available to me head-first. There was a pull-up bar, several dumbbells that went up in weight, and even treadmills, meaning I no longer *had* to run outside in Chicago's below zero cold all the time. I still do every once in a while; (c)old habits die hard.

The months flew by, and before I knew it, Memorial Day weekend arrived. In that intervening time, I spent at least a couple hundred hours in the gym training to undertake what would be by far my most extreme physical and mental test.

The day I decided to do the Murph—the Tuesday following Memorial Day—saw me wake up nervous. It was an emotional cocktail of anxiety, excitement, and fear of the unknown. While I completed each stage of the Murph on its own in my training leading up to the day, I did not do them in a row as is prescribed.

The day began as any other would. I woke up, worked my writing job in the morning, had breakfast, and before I knew it, it was mid-morning, my daily training timeframe. Dressed in a t-shirt, gym shorts, and a pair of tried and true running shoes, I began my journey to the top floor of the building where I would complete each stage.

I did active warm-ups prior to beginning the initial one-mile run. As I did, there was a sudden calm that came over me—it was as if my subconscious was telling my conscious self that everything was going to be okay. I had no idea what I was in for, and it was a blissful state of ignorance looking back.

My first mile went as smooth as could be. Running a mile in about eight minutes to conserve some energy, I made my way briskly over to the pull-up bar. From there, I immediately dropped my butt and began squatting. My station at the pull-up bar and cable machine became my home for the next thirty minutes. Partitioning the challenge into five pull-ups, ten push-ups, and fifteen bodyweight squats as quickly as I could muster was my strategy. While my body was moving, my mind was the true executioner of the Murph.

It seemingly came and went, and after forty-nine minutes and forty seconds, I finished: one mile, one hundred pull-ups, two hundred push-ups, three hundred squats, and another one-mile run. It was hellish. My legs shook, my upper body quivered, and my lungs screeched in agony. I was drenched in sweat, but as I walked on the treadmill to cool down and stopped the timer running on my phone, reality began to somewhat set in. I did it and made a good time.

A tsunami of relief, emotion, and sweat all saw me beat red cooling down on the treadmill. I had done it. I didn't know how to process that I had. My body hurt, and my mind was fried. Yet I still found myself thinking, "I want to do this again."

The following year and on Memorial Day weekend of 2019, I was anxious to do it once more. I planned for the same day as the previous year: June 1st.

The build-up and training were not nearly as concentrated as the year before, however, in that I did not solely focus on the calisthenics and movements I would be doing for Murph. I started to dive into weightlifting and running for cross-training instead. While I certainly became physically stronger, I found myself lagging behind my 2018 pace in the week leading up to Memorial Day 2019.

As the day finally came and I walked upstairs to the same gym I'd completed my first Murph in, I was suddenly nervous. My stomach began to turn and became upset just as I was about to run. *Whatever*, I thought. *I'll push through... but what is going on with me?*

My attempt that day finished three minutes behind my pace from the prior year at fifty-two minutes and thirty seconds. Once again, the experience was hellish, but I left the gym frustrated with myself because I knew I had more to give than what I did. What happened?

I began to make excuses for myself. One was "I must have added muscle this past year, so this extra weight must have slowed me down."

Not quite so. In theory, the increased muscle mass and capacity for cardio through consistent distance running throughout the year should have actually *helped* me. Once I thought about this, I turned to another excuse.

"My stomach cost me today. It just wasn't meant to be."

While my stomach was upset upon arriving at the gym, it was not queasy during the entire morning leading up to my journey upstairs. So, once again, this wasn't quite true.

That day, I had to acknowledge the simple truth: I was nervous. I was fearful that I would not reach the time I achieved the prior year despite all the training I did in the months leading up to the Murph. I found myself stuck in a negative self-talk mode of doubting my every move. This, in turn, drained any reserve energy of mine, and I plodded my way to a fifty-two minute and thirty second finish—a full three minutes slower than my previous year's effort. I folded under my own expectations. This was not me being mean to myself; instead, this was me being bluntly truthful with myself about what happened.

I remained bothered throughout the day and disappointed in myself that I'd let any demons living with me fully take over my mental real estate. It was late that afternoon that I started thinking about trying it again. *No way,* I began to reason. *That's too many squats, push-ups, and pull-ups.* It was in this moment that I thought about David and a credo of his.

Don't stop when you're tired. Stop when you're done.

I was tired, but I wasn't done.

The next day, I woke up wanting to go again. The time moved quickly, and before I knew it, I was fueled up and ready to go for a second round the day after my personal failure.

I practically skipped to the elevators and to the gym. I felt lighter, and it was because of one simple shift: my mindset changed. I shifted from heavy with expectation to open and free. I went in with a clear strategy to tackle the pull-ups, push-ups, and squats: I would keep moving with very little breaks to finish in the best time that I could. Perhaps most importantly was that, because I was now fully present, I was not thinking about hitting or beating a certain time. All I knew was that I would keep moving and see where I ended.

I ended well. My time this second day was a full twelve minutes faster than my previous day. To me, this said everything.

During my first attempt, my mind had taken over me. During my second time, I had taken over my mind. There were moments during that were intensely difficult. I wanted to stop to take a break as I had done repeatedly the day before, but I didn't. Instead, I internally repeated a famed Muhammad Ali quote: "Don't quit; suffer now, and live the rest of your life as a champion."[34]

I did not break any records. My time of forty minutes and forty-eight seconds placed me in the top 15 percent of registered athletes per the official Murph Challenge websites' public leaderboard. This was neat, though it was secondary to my primary discovery: we often are what our mind says we are.

***

I now realize that, with this new lens provided by David Goggins, my life before knowing him from afar was utterly incomplete. It was incomplete in the way that I not only spoke to myself, but would then act upon that dialogue after the fact. I was constantly stuck in a victim's mindset, wherein I was the one being put down by others and myself always. This is not to say that this wasn't sometimes true but that it was truly only sometimes. Plenty of other times, I was to blame for not picking myself up when I knew deep within myself that I probably wasn't going to get it anywhere else.

There is the old saying that goes, "Everyone is fighting a battle you know nothing about. So be kind always." And

---

[34] Muhammad Ali (@MuhammadAli), "I hated every minute of training, but I said, 'Don't quit. Suffer now and live the rest of your life as a champion.'", Twitter, October 15, 2012, 7:52am CST.

throughout my journey, I have found that to be life-changingly true. In the years since meeting David Goggins from a distance, I recognize that my mind's tendency to play the victim of circumstance—thinking I am too overweight, I am not smart enough, I am just not *good* enough—was much more powerful than my conscious brain that knows those refrains to be false. He made me aware of the power of our minds, and how despite the mind's "tactical advantage" over us, we have the ability and the power to wrestle back control.

I am wrestling every day. And I'm sure you are too.

CHAPTER 3

Why We Love Fictional Characters & What We Can Learn from Them

———

Escapism is a powerful tool.

The world has become an enclave for potential mental escapism and distractions. Mobile phones, social media, and the evolution of the all-day news cycle integrated with the meteoric rise of the internet are all enablers for anybody to escape anywhere and anytime. As human beings, we seek this escape to avoid problems within our own lives, and we sometimes do it because we like to dream beyond our present circumstance. Removing oneself from the present moment and transporting to a different location mentally can be as effective as doing so physically.

It is also a powerful way to avoid adverse circumstances. Personally, I know I have spent the vast majority of my life escaping to "better" circumstances that were both real and imagined.

I played pretend a lot as a kid, turning my action figures into living, breathing heroes in my living room. Action figures, dolls, and play sets have the propensity to appeal to the escapist part of our brains. These are items that, while inanimate, can become alive with the power of our minds. The *Toy Story* film franchise is built on this concept, except for that the toys *are* living and breathing beings.[35]

These figurines are often used as vessels into which we pour the imagined lives of others. Famous fictional characters, like the Power Rangers, or even toys specifically given their own personality traits via marketing campaigns, like Barbie or G.I. Joe, have ruled the day. Why? I believe this has to do with the power of fictional characters on our minds, no matter how impressionable or not certain people are while growing up. I was an ultra-impressionable kid, and even now as an adult, I have retained that characteristic, though to a lesser extent. With the ability to live out an alternate reality, we can escape the trials of the real and sometimes cold and harsh world.

This power of fictional worlds and the people that inhabit them cannot be understated. The Marvel Cinematic Universe has grown exponentially in popularity since its 2008 inception. The roster of heroes is often compared to modern day "gods" as the Greeks and Romans knew them,

---

35 *Toy Story*, directed by John Lasseter (2005; Emeryville, CA: Walt Disney-Pixar Animation, 2019), Blu-ray Disc.

prevailing in tales of woe and bringing a sense of assurance and comfort that no matter how bad things may get, all will turn out okay.

This mental escapism through fictional characters and their lives is pursued in the name of comfort. Adversity and pain cause duress and bad feelings in the moment they're happening, so human nature dictates that we seek comfort to escape further pain and punishment. It's what we call the fight or flight reflex of our sympathetic nervous system, and this typically happens when under extreme stress in given situations.

The irony of all of this is that, despite the normal human want and need to actively seek comfort, we relish watching a "hero" overcome pain and obstacles to achieve greatness in both reality and fiction. It is easier to wax philosophic about how tomorrow you will begin your new diet and workout routine but for now can enjoy a fifth piece of pizza. I know because that's what I did.

According to David Goggins, we must approach each day with an open mind and be willing to admit that we *don't* know best in certain circumstances. We must "start from zero" every day, giving great thought to our actions and deeds to expand our minds. Most people fail to recognize the harshness that awaits while deciding to make what should be thoughtful decisions because, sometimes, it just sounds good in that moment. Knee-jerk decisions, while sometimes good when we follow and trust our instincts, often happen from a place of escapism: we want that reality to be true so badly that we fail to recognize the work ahead because we think we know and assume wrongly.[36]

***

I can attest to the pleasure of escapism because I was the king of playing pretend while growing up. Some of my own favorite words as a kid were BAM! POW! Ka-BLOOM! An ardent fan of comic books and their lore, I found their TV corollaries on Disney Channel and ABC Family Saturday morning cartoon blocks enchanting. *Spider-Man*, *Gargoyles*, and *X-Men* were some favorites because within each story the main protagonist or group of protagonists were outsiders. Often misunderstood, they fought for what they believed to be right despite their roles as outcasts.

This was often how I felt. In preschool, before I was self-aware, I would play Power Rangers—another all-time favorite—on the playground. The problem was that I did not necessarily have play mates. I often played by myself and sometimes incorporated others into my faux martial arts routines without their full consent. I got in trouble for this, and rightfully so: the other kids in my class feared getting hurt by my flailing beefy limbs.

I now believe this to have had a profound impact on me. As I grew, I became shyer and more socially introverted. Afraid of getting in trouble, I would do whatever it took to appease those in power; I was a sensitive child who regularly sought

---

[36] David Goggins, *Can't Hurt Me: Master Your Mind and Defy the Odds* (Austin, Texas: Lioncrest Publishing, 2018), 287.

approval from those in charge. In times of adversity or challenge, I would often fold and retreat inward, berating myself mercilessly for, in my mind, "messing up." Being extra hard on myself often finds its way back into my life even today. More than anything during this period, however, I found myself embracing alone time. I had friends, but I also had bullies throughout grade school, junior high, high school, and even college.

Bullying, to me, was upsetting and puzzling. I wondered, why are they choosing me, of all people, to pick on? Am I not big enough to come off as intimidating? I was acutely self-conscious of that latter question because my large frame was often the target of bullies. I have vivid memories of being in my fourth-grade classroom, being made fun of by a table of male classmates for being so overweight that I couldn't make the 'A' league baseball team. Another instance saw a group of high school students drive by my home on a Saturday morning. I was in fifth grade and playing in the front yard. I clocked the car rounding the bend ahead and recognized it as a familiar one that belonged to high schoolers who lived in my neighborhood. Thinking quickly, I hid behind a large fir tree in our front yard so they couldn't see me. I was too late—they saw and sped by, but not before they yelled "FATASS!" and "LITTLE BITCH!" to me.

I needed an outlet as I often felt the weight of bullying (pun intended there) and found trouble coping with the feeling of being completely alone in experiencing it. Football was beginning to become my outlet as a fifth grader, but it was rooted in my everyday life—the very people bullying me were on the football team, often starting alongside me. Instead of lashing out, I turned inward and away, away from the conflict and inward to implore myself to find something, *anything* to help me cope and feel brave.

It was around this time in fifth grade that I found the hero I needed to feel understood. As a half-Italian, half-Irish boy, and with my mom alternating between working part-time and full-time, I spent time at my maternal Italian grandparents' house. Mema and Papa were like a second pair of parents to me as I was growing out of toddlerhood and into young boyhood. Papa had just retired as an inter- and intrastate truck driver in 1991, the year of my birth, and we became intensely close as a result. He would pick me up from preschool and kindergarten, take me to his house where Mema would be waiting with our favorite meal: fresh Italian bread with butter.

My Papa was a veteran of World War II. He deployed to western Europe later in the conflict—late 1944 through the end of the war in early summer 1945. He was proud of his service, though he seldom talked openly about it. He did show me pictures of him as a 19 year old Army private stationed in Switzerland, and I always found it cool to see him as a young man who still looked old to me.

He had a strong moral compass and a quiet confidence about him. His value system of knowing right from wrong and good from evil found their way to me, though not through any deep conversations or reprimands. Instead, it was through his taste in film and TV.

You see, he was *the* biggest John Wayne fan on this side of the Mississippi in suburban Chicago, Illinois. John Wayne, through his storied film career, almost always played the prototypical morally upstanding cowboy out to help the little guy in the romanticized Old West. Papa ate this up.

He introduced me to the almighty Chuck Norris as the titular character on the popular TV show *Walker, Texas Ranger*, which proved another instant favorite for me. He also loved cartoons and introduced me to the superhero shows that were previously mentioned.

His love of TV and movies went beyond the superficial reason of finding entertainment from them. More than anything, he deeply admired the qualities of the movie and TV heroes and protagonists who, through a quietly confident demeanor, led by example. He provided me a living example not only by showing me these shows and movies but also by living with his own quiet confidence and moral uprightness.

As a truck driver throughout the Midwest during the 1950s through the 1980s, he surely had his share of run-ins with law breakers and bandits. He never spoke about this, but his contempt for these people would come out when mob movies like *Goodfellas* or *The Godfather* inevitably came up at family gatherings. His placid demeanor would suddenly turn on its head: still quietly, he would strongly disavow the lifestyles these men lived. Philanderers, murderers, and robbers were the wrong guys to think were "cool." Of course, after first seeing these movies in seventh grade, I was not in the head space to appreciate what he said—Robert De Niro, Al Pacino, and Marlon Brando emanated cool on-screen while doing seemingly whatever they wanted! How is that not awesome to a seventh grade boy?

Easily, according to Papa. It was too easy to be bad and do whatever you want without thinking about consequences. With his guidance, I began to learn that taking the harder route—the route that might cause some pain and discomfort—was worth it. This was a lesson that, while imparted to me while I was young, I couldn't come to fully appreciate until I was in my twenties.

We shared large volumes of time together watching movies and TV, rooting for our favorite good guys. Amongst all these shows and movies, however, there was always one that he seemed most excited to sit down for, even as a sixty- and seventy-something year old man.

Batman: The Animated Series was one of Warner Bros' most popular cartoons at the time, and this status was clear by how many action figures of Batman and his infamous rogues' gallery there were in Target's toy section. Mature, dark, and gritty, it still proves spellbinding to me now as I watch from an adult's perspective. As a kid in need of strong role models that appealed to my sensibilities, it was my nirvana.

On the show, Batman was Bruce Wayne's alter ego. He could become this figure of justice and right in the world, and it could be something that only he knew. During his days, he would appease those around him by playing the role of the socialite billionaire Bruce Wayne, a buffoonish airhead who was also a playboy; however, the depth of the show was found in the reality that Batman and his stance on right vs. wrong was who Bruce truly was at his core. It thusly became one of the first widely consumed on-screen Batman portrayals that postured Bruce Wayne, the air-head playboy, as *Batman's* alter ego.[37]

The Batman mythology is one of the most popular in pop culture and spurs the age-old question for casual and die-hard fans alike: "Who is your favorite Batman actor?" (For me, it's Christian Bale and Kevin Conroy, the long-time voice of Batman on *Batman: The Animated Series*.) When Robert Pattinson was cast to don the cape and cowl in Matt Reeves' forthcoming reboot *The Batman*, he was quoted in an interview with *Variety* as saying that Batman was the only "superhero" he felt connected to growing up.[38] Ben Affleck, Bruce Wayne in 2016's ill-fated *Batman vs. Superman: Dawn of Justice* and 2017's hastily cut *Justice League*, even went so far as to draw a Shakespeare comparison, saying he believed Batman to be "basically the American version of Hamlet." Further drawing on that parallel, Batman will continue to be like Shakespeare's tragic hero because he is continuously conveyed onscreen by actors of the highest caliber.[39]

Rare is it that a mere comic book character reaches this pinnacle of near omnipresence and consistent popularity within the day's pop culture zeitgeist. There was a roughly five-year span following George Clooney's turn as Bruce Wayne in 1997's campy *Batman and Robin* where DC Comics and

---

37 *Batman: The Animated Series*, episode 1, "The Cat and the Claw Part I," directed by Kevin Altieri, written by Jules Dennis and Richard Mueller, featuring Kevin Conroy, aired September 5, 1992, on Fox Kids.
38 *Variety*, "Robert Pattinson Talks 'The Batman'," September 3, 2019, video, 5:30.
39 Keith Staskiewicz, "Ben Affleck: 'Batman is basically the American version of Hamlet'," Entertainment Weekly, July 1, 2015, accessed January 3, 2020.

Warner Bros. shelved the character, but by 2002-2003, prestigious filmmakers began pitching new storylines for Batman to travel across. Christopher Nolan's pitch won WB over, and in 2005, *Batman Begins* hit theaters.

I was once again spellbound. So was the world. By 2008, excitement reached a fever pitch when, prior to its release, *The Dark Knight* earned critical raves, with Heath Ledger specifically earning high praise for his portrayal of the most deviant Batman villain, The Joker. His untimely and tragic passing saw his role take on a larger-than-life aura, especially when those close to him linked it to his work as The Joker. He became the only actor to ever win an Academy Award for playing a comic book-based role, an achievement that still stands as of 2021. There would be one more installment in the trilogy, 2012's *The Dark Knight Rises,* before Ben Affleck was cast for his turn in 2013.

In between these films, various TV shows and new graphic novels were constantly put out to satiate the public's appetite for the Caped Crusader.

I believe Batman's popularity is based in a few elements. The lifestyle of Bruce Wayne, that of a socialite billionaire, is a glamorous one, and people often wish to identify with having an endless supply of money to fuel one's own dream-chasing.

More substantially, however, I believe that at the core of Batman's popularity is his humanity. He exists in the same world built by DC Comics as Superman, Wonder Woman, Aquaman, and the Green Lantern Corps, who are *all* beings with superpowers. Aquaman, Superman, and Wonder Woman are born "special" in that these superpowers exist within them from birth. Hal Jordan, one of the most popular Green Lanterns, has his powers thrust upon him later in life, and while he is not overly willing to accept the mantle of galactic protector at first, he eventually comes around.

Batman is born as a privileged child to philanthropic billionaires Thomas and Martha Wayne and, on the surface, has no superpowers to speak of. His origin story cannot be told without his parents' deaths being front and center as seen in *Batman Begins*. The story often goes that, upon leaving a showing of *The Mark of Zorro*–a darkly-themed opera–Bruce's parents are tragically gunned down in front of the theater by a common street thug during a robbery gone wrong. Bruce is then left helpless with his parents, who lie on the street bleeding out.[40]

This immediate trauma of having witnessed the slow death of his parents follows and haunts Bruce. His life that was once privilege in the embrace of loving, doting parents turns on a bloody dime, and suddenly, he is orphaned and left to the care of his family's loyal butler, Alfred. Here again, he is depicted as the ultimate human: fallible, vulnerable, and outcast. He is so affected by his parents' death that he chooses to devote his life to not only *fight* crime but to completely *rid* his native Gotham City of the crime that infests it once and for all. By setting this goal that is unattainable but altruistic to the utmost, he strives to be the beacon of hope for his fellow Gothamites in a way that he had as a child in the form of his parents.[41]

---

40 *Batman Begins,* directed by Christopher Nolan (2005; Burbank, CA: Warner Bros. Pictures, 2008), Blu-ray Disc.
41 Ibid.

He runs toward adversity and the tough path because of the reward it could yield for him and citizens of the city that he has always called home. He travels the world as a young man, graduating from the best universities money could buy with his genius-level intellect, and begins to study the criminal mind by embedding himself with criminals the world over. He masters chemistry, deduction (a-la Sherlock Holmes), and nearly *all* martial arts. Eventually, upon arriving home in Gotham City to begin his crusade, he needs one final element: a symbol that strikes fear into the hearts of all criminals. To do this, he chooses the dark symbol of a bat—vampiric and rodent-like, a very specific choice.[42]

He chooses the bat because of how intensely afraid of bats he was growing up. His origin story also often includes the anecdote of his accidental fall down a well; upon landing at the bottom, he is greeted by seemingly thousands of screeching bats who attack him from a deeper cave under his family manor's vast grounds. This trauma follows him and is important enough to become what he derives the all-important Batman symbol from.[43]

This story was tailor-made for my struggling fifth grade self. While I did not know a large portion of it at the time, the confidence that Batman exuded on the cartoon and in the comics as he fought against what I saw as super bullies resonated deep within me. As I began to devour the graphic novels, I became a fan of the Batman lore for life.

---

42   Ibid.
43   Ibid.

***

While iterations of Batman see different interpretations of his cowl, suit, sidekicks, or storylines, what has always remained consistent is his deep drive. His unquenchable inner fire to avenge the death of his parents by devoting his life to fighting against what killed them is, I believe, what stokes the fear inside those who cross him and acts as his own "superpower." They know that, no matter what, he will not stop coming for them. His fight is until his death. Bruce knows that, and so do the criminals he fights, and there are no alternative endings.

He reached this dire point because of a singular factor: adversity. Adversity found him with the murder of his parents; he found and sought adversity with his drive towards learning all that he could to fuel his plan of crime fighting, largely on his own, in Gotham City. He put himself through rigors that few would think to undertake while training and learning all that he did. His body suffered, as did his mind and spirit. At the outset of Christopher Nolan's film *Batman Begins* and the rest of the *Dark Knight* trilogy, Bruce is portrayed as utterly lost as he is amid his quest to learn the criminal mind. He cannot cope with the array of emotions he feels as his anger and grief suffocate his inner spirit. It is only when he is offered a helping hand that he turns inward and challenges himself to be better by taking up a stranger's offer to help him on his quest.

He suffers repeatedly, despite being potentially comfortable with infinite wealth and its temptations at his disposal, to achieve what it is he believes at his core is just. He plays the part of Bruce Wayne to appease those around him who know him only as the son of billionaires and a member of Gotham's social upper-class.

This is precisely why Bruce Wayne/Batman serves as a model for what one can achieve through voluntarily facing adversity and suffering. While fictional in existence, the ethos of Batman's character permeates our cultural fabric in so many ways. It is this wrinkle of facing down and eventually embracing adversity, however, that I feel is most important to understanding his widespread appeal and lasting importance.

He is not the only character we could stand to take inspiration from. There are quite literally tens of thousands of characters in the literature, TV, and film canons, with a great many of these being protagonists or anti-heroes. When you see them still standing after life has given them hell, put yourself in their position. How must that feel? I can tell you from personal experience, it is empowering.

READER PROMPT:
Find a quiet place in your home to sit with a notebook and pencil/pen.

Reflect on a fictional character who has inspired you throughout your life. Think about why you enjoyed them and what you identify with in them. Think about how they would approach adversity. How do you think you could stand to take a lesson from them? What about their approach resonates with you?

After your reflection, you can let it sink in: on your ever-evolving journey to bettering yourself, you have just found another ally in your mind to help when things get tough.

CHAPTER 4

Finding a Community

Those were the words of my high school's freshman football coach at our beginning of the season weigh-in. Growing up large—born ten pounds, eleven ounces, and assumed to be twins until the final ultrasound when it was finally deduced that, no, it was just one large baby—was part of my normal. Getting this reaction from a football coach had also become normal. At 6'3" and two hundred and fifty pounds, I was a football offensive line coach's fever dream come to life. Add to that my quick feet, unusual agility for a young man that size, and natural ability to "protect and find the football," and I was surely destined for NCAA Division I football and the NFL.

The problem was that I didn't love the sport. Growing up loved and supported by a tight knit family, I was a sensitive "gentle giant" type who sought to look after classmates smaller than I—not pick on them. I had been picked on despite my size, and I believe now that it was mostly because I would never fight back. Turning the other cheek, shyness, and internalizing my angst was a regular part of my life. The outlet I possessed to channel this angst was, ironically, the football field.

I didn't know how to express that football coaches marveling over my size made me uncomfortable because I was deeply uncomfortable not only with attention but also about the specific type of attention that revolved around my size. I was uncomfortable in my own body, so surely others should be equally as uncomfortable—if not more so—looking at me. My discomfort also stemmed from the coaches' attitudes towards my participating in football and only football. I should be lifting in the offseason and solely focusing on learning the playbook to perhaps become a rare sophomore starter on the varsity squad. The problem—or, one of the problems—with all this was that I had no perception of how to take care of my overweight, oversized body with the correct nutrition and exercise. As a freshman, I still had plenty of baby fat—it made up much of my girth—with a fine layer of natural muscle.

Growing up as a three-sport athlete until my eighth-grade year, I was accustomed to simply *being active* year-round. The concept of training for a specific sport, with a specific weight training program no less, was a foreign concept to me. I was blindsided at the end of my freshman football season when, after a successful start to my high school football career as a starter on both sides of the ball, I was invited to the varsity football team's introductory offseason meeting in January inside—yep—the weight room!

There was a varsity offensive lineman essentially assigned to seeing that I came. His name was James. He had a similar temperament to mine, being a soft-spoken, very large young man who would be a senior on the team the following year. He would approach me in the halls, ask how I was and how I was feeling about football. We would always have a cordial conversation, and he would walk away with me feeling important—the varsity team wants me, and one of the best of the offensive linemen has approached me several times to confirm that! My intention was still to play three sports, and I was excited that one could be at a high level the following year.

I required some physical therapy for patellar tendonitis in my left knee following my freshman year, so this precluded me from any training. I gained some weight and found myself out of shape for basketball—one of my hoped-for three sports. So that left baseball, but long story short, I didn't make the team.

I was part of the first cuts. I was baffled at the time. I did well in my tryout and had been told so by the coaches. It remained a mystery.

The following year, I started on the sophomore football team. We did not fare well as a team, but I again had a successful season in my own right. I had a scary incident during the team's third-to-last game where I was hit viciously on my blindside, knocked nearly unconscious for a split second and taken off the field on a stretcher to an ambulance. Fortunately, there was no major damage, but I was left shaken. I decided to sit out of our final games to the chagrin of my teammates and coaches even though there was no serious physical damage. I was afraid of what had happened and decided I needed to "shake it off."

Following the end of our season and as we cleaned out our lockers, I was approached by one of our team's coaches. He wanted to know if I was committed to the program. I said absolutely I was. The future sounded good to me then, as I didn't have to truly think about football practice for another seven months. The following week, another coach approached me after school and pulled me aside. He, too, asked about my commitment to the program. "You could really go places," he said, "if you just stick with it, get in the weight room, and work." Again, caught off guard, I responded again that absolutely I was committed. He said he'd see me in the weight room. I said so right back.

I showed up to offseason lifting the following week. I feared the weight room and all its frills, of which it had few. I was often in and out quicker than most. My body had a perpetual burn while I was in there, and I was uncomfortable physically, mentally, and emotionally. I did not like that. I did not want to feel uncomfortable.

Two months later, after talking with my parents and having tried my hand at the weight room five days a week, I walked into the varsity head coach's office. We sat down, and I quickly blurted out that I would not be playing football anymore.

"What?! What happened?" he said, taken aback.

It was as if there was a pall that fell over the room in response to my football career's death. I timidly explained that, because of the incident at the end of the season, I was no longer comfortable putting my body at risk. I quit the program, and it was truly only in part for that reason.

The other reason was that I was scared. I was deeply uncomfortable in my own body and trying to find my identity in a

Catholic high school environment that put great emphasis on sports and school. I worked hard as a student but felt a missing portion of myself floating out in the ether. As I left his office, I had a foreboding feeling in the pit of my stomach.

I would go on to again be part of first cuts from the baseball team, once again for seemingly no tangible reason. The football coaching staff stopped looking me in the eye or even acknowledging me, as did the players on the team. In the year after I graduated, I returned for a game in west Chicago with friends. Following the game, the head football coach came over to the sidelines where I was standing with those friends, who were members of the team, and immediately shook all their hands. As I stood in front of him, he pretended I didn't exist with no acknowledgement whatsoever. I was no stranger to this coldness. The year before and as a senior, I applied to be a retreat leader after attending the annual Logos retreat. The man in charge of choosing the leaders happened to be on the football coaching staff; in fact, he was my freshman football coach. I was passed over, becoming one of the only applicants to actively *not* be chosen. By that time, I had lost a great deal of weight—around eighty pounds—and reinvented myself with a singular trait that I had been sorely lacking throughout high school: confidence. So this snub, while stinging some, was not nearly as big of a deal as it could have otherwise been.

A trip to the doctor at the outset of my sophomore year of high school delivered a few harsh realities. My cholesterol count was higher than was normal for a seventeen year old. My joints creaked with regularity, which my doctor attributed to an inactive lifestyle. Most importantly to me, however, he attributed my weight—two hundred and eighty pounds—to that sedentary lifestyle.

Since being cut from the baseball team during the middle of my sophomore year, I lacked any direction or drive for remaining active. Looking back, I can vividly recall the feeling of retreating into myself, away from others and to safety, which usually meant long nights spent on my couch at home. My doctor snapped me out of this reality when he said, plainly, "You're overweight, and you could develop heart disease as a young adult at the rate you're traveling. I think you need to start working out with regularity to lose weight." This sobered me to the reality I had been living in but did not want to acknowledge for fear of the truth: I was self-destructing and leading myself down a path to gross underachievement because of my lack of respect for my bodily health.

My mom and I braved the winter storm outside following the appointment to get to her car. We climbed in, and I was out of breath. We sat quietly in the car as I pondered what I had just been told. As I sat there, I noticed the after-visit summary sitting plainly in the front cup holders. I am still not sure what provoked me to grab it, but I did and was punched in the gut emotionally by what I read.

"Concern that patient is developing high cholesterol and negative health habits, as body-mass-index (BMI) is thirty-six: Extremely Obese."

Tears welled up in my eyes as I saw this as the nail in what felt like my life's coffin to that point. I was spiraling out of control, and I now *knew* it. I spent what felt like an eternity—a couple of months—living with this in my mind's cellar.

I ran for the first time almost exactly two months following my doctor's appointment. What brought me to this point, you might ask? And how did I overcome that fear enough to get into running clothes, step outside, and start trotting? The answer is simple, though this part—putting action to your intentions—often proves the hardest part for people. I know this from personal experience.

***

Our minds have a way of creating noise. When somebody says they are "in their head," that typically means thinking so much you become deaf to your true thoughts. The thoughts that instead begin taking over your mental bandwidth are intruders. Oftentimes anticipation can lead to anxiety, and anxiety can lead to your mind spiraling down a rabbit hole of negativity while presenting you, sometimes with gory details, of seemingly **every** wrong scenario that could happen. Since our minds have lived with us our entire lives, they know our fears. David Goggins has often said the mind "has the tactical advantage" over us due to this.[44]

If you have ever felt this happen to you, you are not alone. I would drain myself of physical energy by falling down these rabbit holes of negativity in my mind. This was the precise state I found myself in when I wanted to start losing weight in

---

44 Tom Bilyeu, "Become A Savage & Live On Your Own Terms | David Goggins on Impact Theory," December 11, 2018, video, 53:41.

high school. My opportunities to be involved in team sports were seemingly taken away for no valid reason. I would only reason later with myself that the football coaches stepped in influencing the baseball team's decision after making my choice to stop playing football. I was not "committed enough" to them, I believe.

Compounding this confusing emotional pain at the time was how I could only make it about one-tenth of a mile before giving up due to intense pain in my hips and shins on my first run. I felt utter despair and resentment towards myself for seemingly getting myself into this mess.

The following week, however, my mindset changed. I ran a few more days, and even despite the intense pain, I made it up to a half-mile without stopping. Momentum is a powerful force, and I created some for myself by continuing to *show up*. A week into running every day, my mindset morphed from one of a victim of circumstance to becoming a champion despite the circumstance. "Nobody can lose this weight for me or magically deliver me to a healthier, more comfortable place," I reasoned, "so it's up to me."

I ran. And I ran. And I ran some more. Running became a painful comfort as it presented an outlet away from school and social dynamics that were ever-present in the small Catholic high school I attended. While running, I did not have to worry about some classmates being cold and mean toward me. I could escape the group of people with whom I'd hung out during my junior year—a group that was mostly, ironically, the baseball team. This confidence I had discovered also introduced a side of myself that, to that point, I had kept hidden: a passion for comedic performance.

Growing up as an enormous *Saturday Night Live* fan and as an observational, introverted child, I often developed my own impersonations of people—celebrities, teachers, parents of friends, and even fellow students. So while running brought about mental peace, performing for people who otherwise would have not paid any attention to me brought an adrenaline rush that could not be replicated. I found another outlet that not only had nothing to do with sports or school but also helped me feel, for the first time ever, that I was being accepted by those who I actively sought acceptance from. Discovering this sensation in high school would prove hugely important in the years to come.

There was a group of guys who drove their own BMWs to school. They hung out with pretty girls. Their default response was a "Hey" when passing in the halls. This came across as cool in high school, even if I now see it for what it *really* was: an overall indifference to me as a person. When I performed, however, they were animated and effusive in wanting me to "do another impression!" Those moments came to define my junior year of high school. I was accepted while performing and undergoing my physical transformation, but not strong enough internally to demand respect as a well-rounded person. I ate lunch and hung around with this group in the mornings before first period but was often mysteriously left off their house party invite lists.

I was hurt by this exclusion. They would talk about it openly in front of me as we sat at lunch, and being the only one there who had no idea about anything they talked about, I often sat quietly. Then, in a seemingly favorable turn of events, they would mention a teacher who I did an impression of, would turn to me to "do it," and I would. Those few seconds were fun. The remaining days spent this way were not.

While this was happening inside of my school's walls, I was working outside of them to become more. I lost eighty pounds between my junior and senior years of high school. My routine consisted of eating less than I burned off, and this was mostly done through running. I discovered the self-confidence I had long been seeking during the summer prior to my senior year. Toward the end of my junior year, I found the gall to separate myself from this group of guys and girls who clearly had little-to-no interest in me. I did this mostly due to my finding a new best friend who brought out the best in me.

Rob was my assigned lab partner, and we hit it off right away by talking about basketball and working out. He spent lots of time in the gym lifting weights because he was on the football team. But you would never be able to tell he was because of his kind and open demeanor. I thought it was awesome that he was a second-degree black belt in Shotokan Karate as a long time martial arts fan and admirer. Mostly, however, he provided a gift I did not know I needed—friendly support and encouragement in the school environment. He was like me in that he was soft-spoken, extremely close to his Filipino family, and mostly kept to himself with a few close friends. His open-mindedness helped me discover that quality within myself, and we quickly found our own group of friends that we would regularly hang out with during our senior year. Rob was the first person I truly hit it off with at my high school, and we remain close friends.

***

In your own journey to self-betterment, the importance of community cannot be understated. People who give selfless and loving support provide an example for us. In the quest to seek out those friends, colleagues, family members, or peers who provide that support, we must open ourselves to new possibilities, new connections, and new experiences. This openness can only come when we love ourselves enough that we are willing to open our worlds up to possibilities outside of our immediate control.

This perpetuates the cycle discussed throughout: to love oneself, we must do a great deal of personal inventory, often alone, to fight and eventually cope and live with any inner demons. Through that process, we become more open to community, external support, and love. Those who remain closed off live a life that has a lid on it—in most cases, this comes from a personal hurt that runs deep. To be a contributing member of a team and to the lives of those who love and support you, you must first learn to love yourself and all your strengths and weaknesses.

Herein lies a paradox: how are we supposed to love our weaknesses? That sounds antithetical, as we are repeatedly told through politics, pop culture, and media—especially those who live in the United States—that those with the strongest strengths are bound to be the ultimate "winners." "Winner" in this context is an ambiguously defined word that somehow means there is victory through the embracing of what makes us strong; however, I would posit through tons of personal experience that this is only half of the integral equation. Those who respect their biggest struggles alongside their biggest successes lay the foundation to becoming well-rounded, self-aware, and ultimately *strong* individuals.

As we learn to accept ourselves and our personal weaknesses, we learn how to become empathetic to others' struggles. That cyclical process plays out most meaningfully from the inside out.

Prior to finding Rob as a junior in high school, I actively sought external validation and befriended others much too easily. What usually happened was that I found myself in uncomfortable social situations that I knew, deep within myself, I did not belong in. Often my actions around others were to gain their approval—this would help me feel better about myself, even if only for a second. As I actively sought others as friends, I very seldom had success in finding those who stuck with me.

Once I took a step back following my junior year of high school, I found myself amid my first massive weight loss and personal transformation. The more I worked on myself by myself, the less I found I needed external validation from the people who gave it to me superficially and usually through laughing at me, which I mistakenly took as laughing with me. My internal validation grew stronger with time, and by the time I was a senior, I naturally found a group of friends who shared my values because of my security in myself.

Alone time is crucial to learning all there is to know about you. Spending time alone not only leaves you with your thoughts but also programs you to go on your journey yourself. For some of us, external support is a luxury, while some are blessed with an overflowing amount. I have been blessed throughout my life to have a small circle of people support me. While knowing that circle would always be there if I need them—and there have been times where I have—I have undertaken and faced down my personal challenges largely on my own. That's because, while the support from my circle is invaluable, they cannot fight my battles for me simply because they are not *me* and living *my* day-to-day life. I am not saying outside support isn't valuable. On the contrary, it is not only valuable, but also necessary. What I *am* saying is that at the end of every day, you must go to bed with yourself knowing what *you* need to do.

As we become more secure with ourselves, we become much more in tune with our values through listening to our internal monologues, thoughts, and feelings. The more work that is done as we are alone, the more likely we are to then deduce *why* we are experiencing those thoughts and feelings, which is integral to being an emotionally intelligent person.

Once we can recognize our own thoughts and feelings and the rationale behind them, empathy for others' thoughts and feelings is much more possible, thus taking the journey from internal to external.

As your empathy for others grows, so too does the openness and courage necessary to insert yourself and your own beliefs into any group. I found that the more I learned to think of others, the less I took myself seriously and found anxiety in everyday life.

This can prove to be a delicate balance for some as you should never feel as if you're drowning while helping others by putting their needs too often before your own. Here is where the importance of being a well-rounded individual comes back into play: throughout that time of taking personal inventory, digging through the mud of my spirit, and immersing myself into the reality of my weaknesses, I have discovered what it was I needed to cope every day. Once you come to this understanding with your mind, you begin to implement this into your everyday life. Upon introducing others' needs before your own, you will know what you need subconsciously as you help.

This might sound like a theory that is too good to be true. If you're thinking that right now, I would encourage you to just try. I have lived it, and throughout the phases of my journey, I have found great fortune in meeting so many others who have gone through the same discovery process.

CHAPTER 5

A Shoe on the Wrong Foot

"It came? It came!"

I sprinted back to my dorm room from my course on US foreign intelligence taught by a former CIA officer in the north quad of Indiana University's sprawling campus. It was the middle of the week of November 2010—my third full month into college—and I had just received word from my mom that a letter arrived in the mail that I long waited for.

She relayed it was a letter with Marquette University's logo stamped boldly to the front, and it did not arrive in a small rectangular envelope. This was a grand 8.5x11 inch package of paper that hinted toward what I had for months longed to know. Was I accepted? Could I transfer?

Before fully getting to that, I should tell you that college did not start as I had planned. As a senior in high school, I flourished academically in courses that were of the level of many university freshman classes. I had a schedule loaded with honors and Advanced Placement courses. For the first time in my academic career, I averaged close to an A for the school year, which was a high watermark of 92 percent at my competitive Catholic high school. I finished at 91 percent. As I planned my next phase of life, I considered what I believed as an eighteen year old would be integral to have in my life for the next four years. I believed a school with Division I sports with high profile games to attend, strong academics, and a fun campus life were all factors to consider. Since I had attended smaller private schools for my entire academic career, I wanted to branch out to a larger public school.

Indiana University Bloomington checked all these boxes: it was a large state school with a strong academic reputation. The summer after high school graduation was filled with trips to Bloomington, Indiana for a freshman orientation program in June, initial placement testing for those proficient in a foreign language, and course selection. Regarding this lattermost category, I was ecstatic. I was planning to major in history/political science, so I enrolled in courses called Leadership in America, Mafia & Other Italian Mysteries, and Intelligence & National Security, which was taught by former CIA intelligence officer Gene Coyle. I had to specially apply to be accepted into this, and to my great joy, I was. This progressive course work was coupled with a fun first few weeks of school socially. I made the university's sketch comedy team, and I felt my college career was off to the best start imaginable.

Then the honeymoon ended.

It took until late September and almost exactly one month into my career as a student to recognize something was off. I no longer felt the fit was welcome; in fact, it felt on the other end of the spectrum. Socially, many activities centered around drinking and rushing to join a fraternity. I drank a couple of times in high school, but I never became a huge drinker. By the start of college, I actively started to gravitate away to pour my focus into schoolwork. It always took me a little longer and a little more effort than others to do my best work, so I felt I should not deprive myself of any excess energy.

I had become disciplined and knew then that I wanted to do so well in school that I would not have a lull in grades to dig myself out of like I did by the end of my high school career. I had gone through the personal journey of losing one hundred pounds within the previous two years and had discovered this "new me" that I loved and wanted to hold at all costs.

I held on to this person as long as I could, but events in my life and the lives of my close friends soon made this more difficult. In my final week of living at home prior to moving for my first week of college, I went for a jog, as had become my daily custom. Running softly on the street, I sought to transition to the sidewalk in my final quarter of a mile leg home. As I did, I suddenly stepped in a pothole, and my ankle snapped outward. I felt a crack accompanied with a burning, shooting pain up my leg. I sat writhing on the parkway, a short distance from my home, but I was in no shape to walk. To my good fortune, there was a neighbor driving by who picked me up, drove me home, and helped me walk to my front door. By the time I arrived home, my ankle looked as if, in my mom's words, "there was a baseball stuck under my skin where my ankle was."

A visit to the emergency room and a set of x-rays later, I was diagnosed with a severe sprain/avulsion fracture with no clear break that otherwise would have required surgery. An avulsion fracture happens when a ligament or tendon becomes so stretched that a fragment of bone goes with it. I received an air cast, one that is removable and contoured to the shape of your leg, and a set of crutches. This all before I was to depart the following week for a Big Ten school whose campus was sprawled over miles of land. I would eventually find that a thirty minute walk to classes without crutches often meant closer to an hour trek with them on the sprawling campus of Indiana University-Bloomington.

By the third week of this predicament, while off my crutches I still possessed a noticeable limp with regular pain in my ankle at any given step. Bloomington is a warm climate, and I am naturally warm myself, so I would often show up to my classes steeped in sweat. My notebooks took a good portion away from my forearms as I attempted to take notes. Physically, it was the most uniquely torturous predicament I had ever found myself in.

On top of this physical quagmire, my third weekend away brought a traumatic experience involving a guy who lived on my floor; let's call him Steve. Steve and I were friendly and got along fine. Within a week, he had found his group of friends—a couple of guys who lived on our floor—and though I began to tag along with them, they became passive aggressive about my reluctance to partake in drinking. They often found excuses to leave me at parties. As all this was beginning to happen, Steve was arrested.

I woke up on a late September Sunday morning to a subdued call from him.

"Hey, Chris... this is Steve..." he started. "I... uh... I'm in jail and I need you to come bail me out. It's a bond, it's set at $1,000, and if you can get it, I'll pay you back."

He was fighting back tears and sounded petrified. I was dumbfounded and shocked myself. I assured him it would be okay, and that I would be on the way with the money in tow. He instructed me on where to go, who to speak with, and how to go about posting his bond. The irony within all this was that I had just been there a week ago myself as part of a school assignment.

My Public Leadership in America professor instructed our class to seek out a local leader for an interview. I sought out the Sheriff of Bloomington, and to my surprise and excitement, he granted me time for not only an in-person interview but also a tour of the Monroe County Jail. After my arrival and a twenty minute question and answer session, we took a thirty minute tour of the jail facilities, which included the "drunk tank." It was a cold-looking room with starkly white-tiled floors, two open toilets, and two benches made of solid stone to lay on. It was simple, and to anyone in my position—a new college student, an effective deterrent of drinking irresponsibly.

This experience played in the back of my mind as Steve described his predicament. I was sure he was there, so I moved swiftly. I knocked on doors and woke up the largely hungover gaggle of guys on my floor. I explained the issue. These were his close friends to that point, and so I felt that they would feel inclined to pool their money together to help him. They were, and within an hour, we had the money to post bond.

We walked the thirty minutes to the jail. I led the way with the other eight or so guys following and murmuring in hushed tones about what could have happened. There were a few who were talking about what they remembered. It did not at all sound like the Steve I had met, but their account would prove true.

The first sign that those few guys were telling the truth came when I saw Steve. I walked carefully into the bail bondsman's office with the envelope of $1,000 on hand. He seemed completely unfazed, having undoubtedly dealt with this hundreds of times before. As I handed the cash over, I filled out some paperwork, and Steve was soon ushered out of the drunk tank from the back. I greeted him at the door, and as I did, I was met with a hug and some tears from Steve. He had a black eye—one he was given while running from police the night before after being caught publicly intoxicated.

I was again shocked to see him in this state: disheveled, bruised all over, and with tears forming an incomplete roadmap up and down his clothes. I led him outside to the group of guys, who immediately gathered around him, patting him gently on the back with assurance that it would be okay. As we walked back, I recognized this as a turning point for me. I had expressed my discomfort to my parents with the college experience at Indiana before, but this drove the point home.

I needed to leave.

That type of drinking, leading one to a truly blackout state where the drinker could not account for their actions after blacking out, was so prevalent that it was frightening to me at the time. I needed a smaller environment, potentially with a religious influence as I had for the previous twelve years of schooling. Coming from a conservative and quiet suburb of Chicago, with a high school environment with as strict a penal code as any, this new loud and lively small town was too jarring to me as an eighteen year old living away on my own for the first time. During my initial discussion about transferring with my mom—one that came a mere two weeks into school, where she suggested that I give it some more time to truly marinate as a new experience—I mentioned Marquette as a possible transfer destination.

Marquette shared a connection to a personal hero of mine: Chris Farley. He graduated from Marquette during the early 1980s en route to becoming a comedic icon of *Saturday Night Live* and meeting a tragically early death at age thirty-three. His biography, *The Chris Farley Show*, became my favorite book during my senior year of high school. How his friends spoke of his time at Marquette—one that was wholesome and filled with a community of people who cared for each other—stuck with me.[45]

It stayed with me as I made the sketch comedy team at Indiana. He was an inspiration as to why I had auditioned in the

---

45 *The Chris Farley Show: A Biography in Three Acts* (New York: Penguin Group USA, 2008).

first place. I was one of three people accepted into the group out of more than thirty who auditioned. I believed I was well on my way to beginning a performing career. This was a prospect that, while personally seen as a long shot at the time, was nevertheless exciting to see it encouraged with my acceptance. I auditioned and made it within my first week of being at school after discovering the team at the annual Organizational Fest held on Indiana's center quad.

But my second week in the group brought about another unpleasant experience. Two of the group's foremost contributors and most popular members were one year older than me, and they seemed elated to have me in the group. We hit it off during the group's first practice that saw us all pitch a sketch idea before beginning to act a few out in a beautiful, ornate event space within the Indiana Memorial Union. It was fun, and the three of us walked for about ten minutes together afterward to bask in the high of a successful session of sketch pitching.

They told me all about the party at their house set for the coming weekend as a welcome for me and the two other new members. As I continued the final ten minutes of the walk by myself, I relished my relationship with them, even if I was uneasy about the others' attitudes toward me. There was a coldness from the older members of the group seen through little-to-no acknowledgment of me upon showing up to practice, their blasé attitudes while I pitched my sketch ideas, and the use of bits I created on my own as we performed as if they had come up with them. Despite this, the treatment of me by the two popular members of the group helped assuage any concerns I had.

The week flew by in anticipation. By the time Friday arrived, I was dressed and ready to go at five p.m., when I was told that I could walk over to their house. It was a twenty minute walk, and I walked rapidly to keep the nervous anticipation forming in the pit of my stomach at bay. I arrived, and to my surprise, was the only one there. They had invited me over for us three just to hang out. They were so excited to see me. It was unlike anything I had experienced before, and for once, I felt completely accepted by older students. Furthermore, my talent in performing comedy felt validated because of this amazing treatment.

After about an hour of sitting, nursing a beer, and talking about my background in both comedy and life, we drove to the nearby grocery store in Bloomington to pick up the stockpile of alcohol for the night. We squeezed in the other two new members on the way home, and soon enough, the party began. The liquor and beer filled the entire back of their car, and they could not be more ecstatic for the fun sure to come.

With the senior members arriving shortly thereafter, it was beginning to be a fun time for all. I enjoyed people-watching while nursing just two beers to stay sober. Being that these were people I did not know very well, I wanted to keep my wits about me.

Around one a.m., I stood outside with a then-drunk senior member. He was one of the seniors who was not overly kind. The other senior member became more animated with alcohol and was kinder to me that evening, but not this guy. He went from animated to stoic as I stood next to him on the back porch. We were a couplet within a larger grouping, and suddenly, he began to talk. I remember little about the conversation before he said, "Honestly, I didn't really want to cast you, but [the two popular members] really wanted you, so we relented." There was a lull, and within a few seconds, we parted ways, and I began my walk home.

I was crushed. On the one hand, it was flattering to know that the two members who had spent so much time trying to get to know me were derived from a genuine interest. On the other, it was disappointing to hear what I had suspected: this senior member, and presumably a few of the others judging by his use of the word "we," did not *really* want me in the group. In fact, it sounded as if they'd campaigned to *not* accept me. I was unwanted by potentially more members of the group than by those who wanted me, and their disinterest seemed hostile. To that point, my experience at Indiana was uneven. This started to prod it down the road toward miserable, and it was the next day that I started seriously researching a transfer to Marquette.

***

For the first time in my life, I began to feel what would become clinical depression. Waking up that following morning still brought about the feeling of a hangover despite the fact that I did not drink enough to achieve one. I was distraught and suddenly felt completely out of place. It was like I was trying to fit a shoe onto the wrong foot. I went from feeling lukewarmly in as a student to completely out. In retrospect, I recognize that what I was feeling then was like what I felt as I began to work out after leaving Marquette. My soul and my psyche felt out of shape. I was not at all prepared to cope with adverse circumstances during a major life change, let alone cope solely with that major life change. This was mostly due to how isolated I felt.

People battle with being cast out or isolated all the time. While I was a student at Indiana, it became my norm. On a campus of sixty thousand plus students, it was crushing to feel truly alone amongst all those people. Those who have experienced that know just how much of an out of body experience it can become. Sometimes you forget that you exist and instead become an observer of how important everybody else is. For my part, I would often get down on myself for not sticking up for myself and going into a shell when confronted with a bully or an adverse "real life" situation. This brought about negative self-talk that fueled my isolationist tendencies.

The only real company I had then was my family and especially my mom. We spoke on the phone nearly every night, including weekends, and often for long periods of time. I was homesick, but she and my dad were so steadfast in their support of my getting through at Indiana while feeling cast out.

In the years since Indiana, I have dealt with many experiences where I still felt completely alone and without a reliable support system. At various times, I felt as if I was the only person experiencing the despair and loneliness that comes with being isolated, especially within the context of a larger group. My discovery that has since helped me cope with these feelings—which still percolate my mind every now and then—has been actively working on my self-talk.

I define self-talk as what you say to yourself in the context of the ever-running inner dialogue happening inside your head. You know yourself, and so you should hypothetically be completely in control of self-talk, but we often have different voices in our heads, telling us different things. This is especially true in dark times; therefore, feeling bad for ourselves becomes very easy, and devolving into the "victim" becomes even more tempting.

The legendary and controversial World War II Army General George S. Patton instructed his troops, "Fatigue makes cowards of us all."[46] As somebody who was depressed, lonely, and truly isolated, I can attest. I found that my level of fear and anxiety rose as my fatigue and negative self-image deepened. On top of my brain's chemical imbalance, this began to happen because the quality of my self-talk deteriorated and sometimes disappeared completely. I was often left feeling as if I had to fend for myself because nobody had my back—not even me. This ratcheted up those feelings of anxiety and depression.

What I found, however, was that the more I talked positively to myself, the more likely I was to feel empowered.

In my experience, to do this you must begin by first recognizing the quality of your thoughts. This takes deep introspection and time spent by yourself, often in a quiet room. We as humans have the intellectual capability to observe our passing thoughts. Sometimes this observation feels easy,

---

46 *Military Essays and Articles*, ed. Charles M. Province (San Diego, California: The George S. Patton Jr. Historical Society, 2002), 65.

like watching a raft on a lazy river, or nearly impossible, like trying to identify a single passenger on a passing train. To slow that mental train, we must first gain control back over our minds—deep breaths and the acknowledgment simply of *where you are* in that given moment help with grounding us in the present reality. I have discovered through my own experiences that it then becomes about us—*Why was my mind racing like that?* or *Why am I talking to myself so poorly?*

I once heard a professor say something to the effect of we would never speak to other people the way we sometimes speak to ourselves. Because this negative dialogue happens inside of our own heads, it feels less real; once its verbalized, however, it takes on its own life.

David Goggins taught me another method for how to effectively employ this in everyday life. He has what he calls his own "cookie jar." In it, he says, are all his achievements and accomplishments. It rests comfortably in his mind. When participating in a particularly grueling event, he will undoubtedly begin to want to quit; with his cookie jar, however, he reminds himself of what he has done before and uses these "cookies" to power through the adversity.[47]

You deserve to remind yourself of just how far you have come. The journey is what makes any end product worth the time, effort, and sometimes great personal tax that come along with striving for greater and better.

---

47 David Goggins, *Can't Hurt Me: Master Your Mind and Defy the Odds* (Austin, Texas: Lioncrest Publishing, 2018), 187-190.

***

Along with self-talk, the isolation and yearning to strive for more forced me to live outside of my comfort zone. After I began researching Marquette's application process for transfer students, I concurrently planned a time to visit the campus. I was fortunate to know many students from high school—including close friends, like Rob—who chose to attend Marquette from the get-go. In the week leading up to my visit, I called a few of them, asking each what I could expect. Mostly, I wanted to hear how amazing it was there and how *different* it was from Indiana. For the most part, the more I heard, the more I was convinced that I was going to love it there.

I traveled with my dad and two friends from high school to visit during fall break of my freshman year. My dad, friends, and I were all up early the next morning, and we made the comfortable one-and-a-half-hour drive to Milwaukee. This was already a few steps above my Indiana experience as the ride to Bloomington was at least four hours. The sights alongside the highway to Milwaukee even felt more comfortable with more industry and suburban surroundings permeating my every glance. The rural drive to Indiana was permanently put to shame in my mind.

We exited the highway on an off-ramp that resembled a luge with a drop of thirty degrees before a turn back upward leading to Wisconsin Avenue, Marquette and Milwaukee's central street. We soon turned left onto Wisconsin, and the stark white stone gates welcoming visitors to Marquette immediately greeted my eyes. We slowly made our way through them in light Friday traffic. Just like that, we were there.

I was shocked, however, because I was surprisingly blasé about what I saw with the campus. There was nothing that immediately struck me as home. It was not love at first sight. The further we drove, the more internally anxious I became.

"This needs to be it!" I told myself.

My dad dropped my friends off at their dorm as we drove to the nearest parking garage to leave the car for the day. We parked and soon after made our way to the Alumni Memorial Union in the middle of campus. We took it all in. It was a gorgeous fall day with a potpourri of leaf colors and a brisk breeze lining our walk to the union, but I remained neutral, and after having lunch in the union, my dad and I decided to walk campus.

At Indiana, I remember noticing just how many students my age wore sweatpants, sweatshirts, and flip-flops around campus and to class. This was a culture shock to me because I'd come from a high school in which every male student wore a tie, and the young women donned skirts with tights. The shirts and tights were both polyester and not optional during the scorching summer and early fall months. This dress code matched the school's environment: rigid.

At Marquette, one of my very first observations was that many students wore jeans, which were largely forgotten at Indiana. I have nothing against those who prefer the total comfort of sweatpants; it was just never my personal style. Noticing this trend introduced to me the concept of home and familiarity with a college experience. The visit proved meaningful. My first night back at Indiana saw me dream about Marquette's campus. The more I walked around Bloomington, the more resolved I was to push on to make it through to Marquette my second semester.

As I sat with my big Marquette envelope in late November of my freshman year, my heart raced at the speed of a perennial NASCAR champion. Three months of hard work, a divided mindset, and much internal strife came down to this singular moment. My calls home in tears played in my mind.

After a solid minute of just sitting, I moved to open the envelope. Among the first sheets of paper was one resembling a letter. All I saw was, "Congratulations, Christopher!" and I yelled in utter joy. I checked back almost immediately to make sure that this was not a prank and read the letter's entirety. I was accepted into Marquette as a full-time transfer student for the coming spring semester. A wave of relief, accomplishment, and resolve washed over me.

My transfer went as smoothly as could be. I earned all fifteen credits of Indiana coursework despite the uniqueness of the courses I'd taken because Marquette went out of their way to find comparable courses. My first semester, while bumpy at first, saw me eventually blossom in ways that I had always wanted to.

I began going out with friends. I mentioned earlier that my close friend, Rob, from high school was a student there, so I spent many waking hours outside of class with him. We would go to the gym, and it was there that I learned how to operate weights. Rob taught me *how* to train effectively to become stronger. Unlike my high school experience, I embraced it there as I felt fully safe in an environment that was not my high school weight room.

As my confidence grew, so too did my friend group. For the first time in my life, I spent months in relationships with two different young women. At the end of my freshman school year, I was still in a relationship with the latter of these two. We had hit it off and begun seeing each other through mutual friends. We made plans to remain in touch and see each other as often as possible throughout the summer apart. She was from the Green Bay, Wisconsin area, and I lived forty-five minutes southwest of Chicago.

I spent one weekend at her family's home in Green Bay cheering her on in the Green Bay Marathon. I arrived with flowers and sweets and was welcomed warmly by her family. It was a wonderful weekend where quality time with just us and her family was the priority. I left not quite believing where I was in life. In a span of a few months, I went from out of my element at Indiana to fully in it at Marquette. I found myself truly happy.

I worked a landscaping job throughout the summer and remained in touch with the young woman whose family I'd just met. We made plans for her to come and visit my family over a weekend in late July of that summer following my early June visit, and we left one another excited at this prospect.

In the intervening time, however, she inexplicably became more distant. An uncle to whom I grew up very close passed away unexpectedly, and I found myself affected profoundly by it. Despite my own grief, days would go by before she would answer my texts. Seldom was it that she picked up her phone to talk. By the time she came to visit Chicago, she was fully cold and distant. She came and left in one fell swoop, and I did not hear back from her the rest of the summer. The most I got was an impersonal "Happy Birthday!" text on my birthday in late August and at the beginning of the school year. I began that school year with a foul taste in my mouth and a troubling trend of sleeping for long periods of time and often.

As I visited the doctor prior to returning to school and described my symptoms—always tired, disinterested with an actively racing mind—he listened, and without any real diagnosis, he prescribed Celexa, an anti-anxiety medication. He also prescribed that I take part in a sleep study at a nearby sleep institute, where there was eventually nothing found to be wrong with my sleep habits. Not knowing anything at all about mental illness or that the drug I was prescribed was used to treat clinical depression, I left our visit grateful that he'd given me medicine that should help.

My dad and I drove back up to Marquette the Sunday following my appointment. He spoke with me in a hushed tone when my new medication came up and told me that I didn't need to tell anybody that I was taking it. There was no need to flaunt it—I can know that I have it, and that can be it. I entered this conversation about mental illness knowing very little, and I left with the stigma that it should be kept hidden and not talked about. We have discussed this exchange in the time since, and while this was not his intent, I took it completely seriously.

Discussing mental illness is certainly a tricky task. Every individual's chemical makeup is different and unique. There is no right or wrong way to treat any illness of the mind, and different routes work for different people.

If you ever find yourself experiencing extreme feelings associated with mental illness, the first task should be to seek professional help.

I discovered this as I made an appointment with a Marquette counselor during the week following my medication prescription. As a specialist in mental health, she seemed to check the box in what I needed—somebody to talk to about my life experiences that I believed then were causing me trauma. My fatigue was leaving me anxious, and my mental health seemed like it was deteriorating. Our session lasted the promised hour, but it seemed to come and go without any real listening. With no real emotional connection to her stoic and cold demeanor, I left disappointed in my experience. Within the span of a couple of weeks, my perception of mental illness changed drastically. I went from not having a fundamental understanding to seeing my own struggle as not *really* mattering. Its status as something that should not be discussed and that could not hold the attention of a seasoned therapist spoke volumes.

This experience wrecked me. In the years following, I made no effort to seek out any counselor or therapist because of how negatively I was affected during the session. I came to see my journey solidified as one that I was on alone with no external help. My instance with this counselor proved to be another watershed moment for me because losing trust in medical professionals while on the downward slope of depression left me feeling as if I was shouting into a void.

The beginning of my sophomore year was already off to a shaky start with the negative counselor experience. I would soon discover that, while the next couple of weeks would bring about immediate joy in making the campus improv. comedy group, this would prove to be a more traumatic experience than fun one.

CHAPTER 6

Delaying Gratification

Your parent or parental figure calls from the first floor of your home. You sit up in your bedroom, pretending to be busy with anything at all, anxiously awaiting this call.

"Cookies are done!"

You rush to the kitchen, smelling the delicious baked dough coupled with a cacophony of other flavors—cinnamon, or chocolate, or even cooked oats. Bee-lining to the stovetop, you grab for the cookie closest to you as quickly as you can. You devour the cookie. You reach in for another. You devour that cookie. Before you know it, you are four cookies deep with seemingly no end in sight.

After your *nth* cookie, you come down from your euphoric high and inevitably wonder, sometimes aloud: "What now?"

Sometimes you go in for that fifth cookie. You might comfortably make your way to the refrigerator and pour yourself an ice-cold glass of milk. You were supposed to have dinner with friends in about an hour, but that's okay—you can find something simple and "healthy" when you're out, you reason in a moment still filled with cookie elation. It will be fun to socialize with friends, too. This whole scene lasts not more than two minutes, and you have downed four cookies while still thinking about having a fifth because why not?

After you've let your mouth watering run its course, consider this scenario.

There is an adult in the kitchen, working away making cookies. You sit upstairs in your room or office, working away on a pertinent project. It is late afternoon time, just before you are to eat dinner. An announcement is made from the kitchen that the cookies are done, and dinner should be here in about an hour. You give an affirmative "Okay, thank you!" and you continue to work on your project.

You eventually make your way downstairs and have dinner with family and friends. Soon after dinner ends, the adult who did the baking makes their way over to the stove, gets the beautifully displayed serving dish of double chocolate chip cookies, and brings them over. You take a dessert plate, two cookies, and place them in front of you. As you go in for the first bite, you allow yourself to remember, "I actually had two pieces of birthday cake yesterday." After a short internal deliberation, you put both cookies back on the serving dish, deciding to remain loyal to your rule of "one treat night per week." You sit and enjoy the company of those around you, knowing you will have a treat night next week to look forward to.

***

There is nothing inherently *bad* or *wrong* with either of these scenarios. Growing up, I was most often the kid in the first scenario; however, there is a major difference that I have found not only worth exploring, but to be integral in optimizing my mindset toward every commitment in life.

Nearly every high achieving person I have had the good fortune to study or know adheres to the concept of delayed gratification. Its gist is as simple as it sounds: you delay gratification or satisfaction as long as is possible before allowing oneself to finally take part and revel in the feeling of gratification in any situation where it is possible.

This concept finds its root in the human mind. We are mentally programmed to seek positive experiences to feel comfortable and safe. Oftentimes these positive experiences endow us with a sense of gratification that brings about feelings of euphoria, contentedness, and overall happiness. We have a neurological response wherein our brain releases endorphins, often alongside oxytocin, serotonin, and dopamine, the four chemicals which make up our brains' "happiness" emitters, and thus can feel that gratification and contentedness deeply and meaningfully.[48]

In the Declaration of Independence, the founding fathers of the United States put forth what they felt were every human's inalienable rights: life, liberty, and *the pursuit of happiness*.[49]

---

[48] Crystal Raypole and Dr. Timothy J. Legg, "How to Hack Your Hormones for a Better Mood," Healthline, accessed January 2, 2020.

[49] Thomas Jefferson, et al, *The Declaration of Independence*, July 4, 1776, manuscript/mixed material, The Thomas Jefferson Papers at the Library of Congress.

In the modern world, many people live unhappy existences with more stressors than ever. The annual Gallup Global Emotions Report found that the US ranked as the seventh most stressed country in the world in 2018-2019.[50] When opportunities for some immediate gratification present themselves—no matter how superficial or slim that gratification might be—people are often eager to take it. This nebulous pursuit of happiness spelled out by the founding fathers thusly becomes less of an ongoing pursuit and more of an "I'll take it when I can get it," moment-to-moment existence. Here is where the two above scenarios come back into play.

The irony behind all this is that those people who do often "take it where they can get it" do so often and find *plenty* of that superficial type of gratification. Food, alcohol, video games, TV, movies, and on the more severe end, drugs, give a quick "high" that usually does not last beyond that singular experience. In fact, there are even times where we get down on ourselves after each experience because of how much was drunk the night before or how much we ate in a fit of hunger. This is the first cookie scenario above: your overwhelming and often emotional desire for a cookie, or four, overtakes the rest of your mind that would tell you otherwise. Our brain takes on a white noise-like quality where all we hear are sweet nothings from the part of our brain that craves these highs: "You deserve it," it whispers. "Just have a few, and imagine how *amazing* it's going to taste."

What most people don't realize is that we *do* have control over that part of our brain. Once we discipline our minds

---

50   *2019 Global Emotions Report.* (Washington, DC: Gallup, Inc., 2019).

to enable delayed gratification, the experiences that do bring about happiness and personal satisfaction prove far and away more lasting and more substantial than the examples above.

Now more than ever, "quick fixes" are around every corner. Have a flabby belly but want a six-pack in time for summer? No matter that you have a month until "beach season!" There are companies that will market you their girdles promising a groundbreaking muscle activation in the core muscles that blast away that pesky fat and, defying science, raise your abs to the surface fully defined and already oiled to show off. Want to ace your exam on Dante's *Inferno*? You're covered there, too, with SparkNotes summarizing and simplifying each passage en route to becoming a student's best friend. You might do well on that exam, but you won't have carried anything with you or genuinely learned.

I was guilty of using these when I did not need to as a student. CliffsNotes and simplified Shakespeare books were sometimes my best friends as an English major in college. I now see how I missed out simply because of laziness and desire for immediate answers and satisfaction. In addition, I have repeatedly been guilty throughout my life of emotionally eating, which often masked deeper and more substantial issues with my mental, spiritual, and physical health.

When we delay gratification, we are consciously choosing to tell ourselves, "Not now." It is not a forever "No" even if it sometimes *feels* that way, which is precisely the point. It might *feel* that way, but brash emotional responses have a way of diluting reality. Recognizing this takes practice, as does becoming adept at delaying your gratification. For you to feel the full positive effect, it must become part of your *everyday lifestyle*. It is not something that one can choose and not choose at random. One must train their mind to begin thinking and subsequently acting this way as a default mechanism.

Here, again, is where practice takes precedence over further education. My wife and I talk about this often. Sometimes when we have a list of chores or tasks ahead of us, seeing the full list can overwhelm our minds. We see the list with its length running down the page, start thinking about conflicts and how we can *possibly* make all this work, and before we know it, we have now fallen down a mental rabbit hole to climb out of, and we are not actually working. Our human minds are not made for so much stimulus, and so it is a human reaction to become overwhelmed when priorities become conflicting and muddied.

Occasionally, emotions dictating action on their own leads to positive outcomes. This is more of an open proposition because when one makes an emotional decision impulsively and without any semblance of reasoning, the chances of success are, at best, a fifty-fifty proposition.

You might also be thinking, and rightfully so, that delaying gratification for too long, or too extremely, can lead to even worse indulgence than before. This is precisely why practice and getting to know yourself are so integral to delaying your own gratification. By knowing what makes you tick, you will be much better equipped to approach each situation with a balanced, unemotional mind. Again, we must acknowledge the inherent truth to bettering oneself; it is an ongoing, non-linear journey that will have bumps in the road. While these bumps might be difficult in the short term, they will only benefit you in the long term by serving as learning experiences.

This all *sounds* amazing, but how do you actively employ this and start to embed it into your everyday lifestyle? The importance of setting small goals cannot go understated. There is an advantageous power to finding smaller goals while pursuing the larger, more overarching purpose. You might have even heard this before and thought, "*That* sounds great, but how?"

My wife loves making to-do lists the old-fashioned way, with a pen and paper. She says that all the information swirling around in her head becomes tangible the moment she physically translates it to a sheet of paper with her hands. A pen and paper are more immediate and less detached from us than the digitized computer screen that stares emotionless back at us. Our personalities are in our handwriting. There is art and emotion in the creation of any handwritten words.

On top of this attractive familiarity through handwriting, you will have already accomplished something simply by making a to-do list. In my experience, when one creates personal momentum, one has a much better shot at continuing.

My wife says that once she has made the to-do list and tangibly sees the information on the to-do list, ordering and prioritizing tasks becomes easier because the information is immediately accessible and therefore able to be ordered and reasoned with. Having nebulous floating tasks in our heads can befuddle us and lead to paralysis by analysis; too much thought can render even the most efficient person helpless.

This method of making a to-do list has helped my wife and I many times. Over the course of our relationship, we have used these to break larger goals down into smaller ones; however, we also need to acknowledge that everybody handles stress and tasks differently. In recognizing this, we can also face what can be a hard truth.

You just need to start. Go. Jump.

Paralysis by analysis happens much too often and to so many people. Even if one isn't suffering from this in their quest to achieve what they would like, it usually means that one is procrastinating, delusional, or just avoiding the truth altogether instead. I have been guilty of each.

Once you are moving, you will find that your momentum is what will keep you going. Focus not on your end goal but instead on what you need to do that day (or what needs to be accomplished that hour or simply that minute). Smaller goals will accumulate over time. As they do, you will recognize that accumulation. If you personally are having trouble recognizing it, then those within your immediate circle and support system will be there to remind you. This is one of the many reasons why having a loving and genuinely caring support system is integral to seeing your journey through: they will have your back as you learn to have yours.

You should remember that the journey continues. It takes an immense amount of practice toward integrating these momentum-building strategies into your everyday life and lifestyle. The Academy Award-winning actress Octavia Spencer, in her commencement address to the 2017 Kent State University graduating class, imparted these words of wisdom: "Treat triumph and failure just the same."[51] These are moments that happen along the journey of discovering your true self and defining your character. Your accomplishments and failures are not the finish line, but they are check points on the larger journey of your life.

READER PROMPT:
- Think about your day tomorrow.
- Write down everything you want to accomplish in no particular order.
- Examine the list, considering your consistent daily priorities, like your job, your family, any extracurricular plans, etc.

Pick your top three to five tasks that you want to accomplish. Frame your day to specifically carry out the tasks that you have just written down. These are now your priorities for solely that one day. If you finish and find yourself with extra energy, do another task.

See if you can create some momentum for yourself with your own to-do list.

---

[51] *NBC News,* "Octavia Spencer's Kent State Speech 2017 Commencement (Full)" May 31, 2017, video, 23:47.

CHAPTER 7

"More... Toned."

I anxiously dialed to call my mom as I hung up on my previous call. In one fell swoop, and seemingly in the same breath, I spoke eagerly.

"Mom..." I led, "I have some news..." She didn't bat an eye, and her voice was unchanged.

"The internship?"

My excitement, about to burst, was suddenly dampened. "Well... yes! How did you know?"

Her response brought it all back. "Because it's you. I am so proud of you!"

I was accepted into a prestigious theatrical internship in the final months of my collegiate career at Marquette. The internship would involve understudying every one of the theater's main stage productions, and shadowing actors of a Broadway and West End caliber. It seemed like all my dreams were coming true all at once. Besides this, I began my journey to bettering my health by going to the gym about two weeks prior to finding out about my acceptance. I was more driven than ever to continue.

While the drive seemed like a good thing, it proved to be anything but that. I was so focused on performing that I neglected my studies. Performing took over my life in ways that were so detrimental that I still feel their effects even now. The toxicity of each environment I found myself in coupled with the overt bullying from those who were so-called friends helped me right into the dark path I was already leading myself down. Allow me to set the scene.

***

My psyche and my soul were shattered. I have since discovered that a major through line for my life has been a deep desire for acceptance. I wanted so badly to be accepted into a social circle that I was proud of. At Marquette, I believed that I found that. Making the improvisational comedy group and finding success on the theater's main stage brought about a feeling of intense validation and sense of self. This was my calling, and not only did I have the gumption to become involved with it, but I thrived within it. For the first time ever, I had peers and teachers alike—some of whom were not performing arts professors but had simply gone to a production with their family or taken the show in on their own—openly telling me how talented I was, how much they believed I should continue. These were sentiments that felt different than the football coaches in high school. They really *mean* it, I reasoned.

With time, however, I found that these words often rang hollow, and it was for the same reason that I saw the football coaches employ. These people were not attached to me as a well-rounded individual. There was an attachment to some potential or some nugget of talent that I possessed, but that is where any care began and ended. I took words and surface-level actions as deep, genuine care because I knew that was my feeling, too. Friends became acquaintances, and acquaintances became bullies within the span of two years. I went from a nice story within the theater department to a threat and competition for the department's majors, who were at Marquette solely to study and perform theater.

I began to seek out stories of famous performers who suffered from depression and anxiety and came to find that a great many famous comedians and actors have talked openly about their struggles. I would find refuge in Robin Williams stand-up specials or vintage Chris Farley films—their escapism through performing while dealing with intense mental health issues was inspiring to me. I saw myself as doing the same: abandoning my own personality at the door of the theater in favor of whichever character I was playing at the time. My obsession with performing and the arts grew deeper as time went on because it was an outlet that let me out of dealing with my own issues. That was a problem that I could not see at the time; it was easier to see myself as a victim and revel in the depression and anxiety.

I now see just how dangerous the glorification of mental illness can be.

The then-friends of mine who bullied me often did so in passive aggressive ways. I was seeing the world through a fogged lens, so even if I knew in my gut the moments where I was being bullied, I could not rationalize it because I did not want to. My junior year became a fight for relevance in the theater department because I feared that I had lost the acceptance I thought I had. By the time I began my senior year, I was roughly seventy-five to eighty pounds heavier than at the beginning of my sophomore year with hundreds of more pounds psychologically and spiritually bearing down on me.

The summer prior to my senior year saw me take a five week intensive course with my closest friend, Mike, from the college improv. group at a prestigious improv. comedy theater in Chicago. We were even cast in the same ensemble. Of nine total groups, we somehow ended up in the same one. Over the two years together in the campus improv. group, we became close; we often discussed how both of us grew up feeling like outcasts until meeting one another. He was talented, I always had fun performing with him, and together we seemed poised to take Marquette comedy to new heights.

We enjoyed a successful five weeks at the intensive, met a wonderful group of people, and performed in our graduation showcase to great reviews from our teachers. They were instructors and performers themselves at the theater. One of our cast mates even pulled us aside and suggested that we develop a two man improv. show. We were elated and set to start the year on a high note.

That did not happen. Our first week of improv. practice back at Marquette saw Mike clash with the presidents of the group.

He asserted, somewhat confrontationally, that we were putting on our own show, and that was final. I stood sheepishly behind him as the conversation devolved and became contentious. The three presidents of the group were my age but had seniority over me since they had been on the team longer than I had been. They loved the group and felt a great possessive ownership over its smooth operation. I went out of my way to be non-confrontational and was always friendly with the three.

Mike took it upon himself to be overly confrontational and assert our show's validity. "I just didn't want you to leave it up as an open-ended question and be too nice, so I thought, 'I'll be bad cop here,'" Mike later told me. It turned out that this confrontation wasn't needed, however, as the presidents of the group immediately acquiesced. They were even encouraging. So we *would* be putting on our two man show even with this tense beginning.

Mike's dismissiveness towards me continued throughout the semester. As we geared up to put our show on, homework often fell by the wayside as I allowed the show to become a higher priority. I feared Mike's attitude going into our two person practices, as it would often be only us. He was abrupt in sharing his thoughts on scenes we would perform and routinely questioned decisions I made. We were fortunate to have guests sit in on a practice a couple of times, and there were a few campus publications writing pieces featuring interviews of us. Despite this, he was often even more critical in front of the guest and made passive aggressive remarks that were passive only to him. It was the first time since junior high school that I ever felt truly nervous around somebody who I considered a close friend.

During the evening lead-up to the third and final show of ours, I became ill. During time that was supposed to be dedicated to having dinner in Milwaukee with visiting family, I instead found myself doubled over in pain. My head pounded, my stomach swirled, I broke out in a cold sweat, and felt faint as dinner wound down. I was not throwing up, however, so me, my family, and friends at the time dismissed it as exhaustion from the intensive rehearsal and performance schedule. I now know it was because of how physically anxious I was to see Mike at the theater again.

That following February, I left the campus improv. group because I needed a mental and emotional break. Mike was openly supportive of this decision and felt that I could use it. After a week, I arranged a sit-down for the presidents of the troupe, myself, Mike, and one other member to hash out any differences. I spoke as openly and honestly as I could muster. By the meeting's conclusion, we hugged, agreed to move on, and left with progress made. On the walk home, however, Mike was conspicuously silent. I attempted to make conversation, but he did not reciprocate save for short one-word answers and eyes askance of my own.

This pattern of disregard by Mike continued for the next three months. He openly ignored me. He did not speak to me at our bi-weekly practices. One instance that has always stuck with me happened a week following this meeting. As I walked home from the campus 7-Eleven following our improv. practice, I spotted him talking to his then-girlfriend, whom I knew well, in a dorm lobby. His back was to the windows as he leaned over the front desk, animatedly talking to her. She saw me coming from across the street as I crossed to say hello. She whispered in his ear while maintaining eye contact with me, and rather than turn to greet me, he concertedly remained with his back to the windows. She then turned her head askance, as if I were a ghost quickly passing through. It was as if, for a moment, I did not exist.

I called my younger brother while choking back tears. I had never done that before. My reaction to this behavior was immediate anger that soon turned to guilt. I felt I had done something to anger him and that I had deserved this. It did not take long for my brother to quash that theory because he was appalled by Mike's behavior. He talked me through it and told me it was going to be okay, providing a voice of reason to let me know that this was *not fine*.

I *know* that I am not the only one to have experienced the intense feeling of loneliness when being bullied by those deemed to be my close friends. It's a nearly impossible dichotomy to match up logically. In my experience, however, I found that in the end, bullies are bullies. It may take time to recognize this. It took me three years to feel as though I had reconciled that Mike was a bully in friend's clothing, but you can find solace in knowing that, with your own personal growth, this closure will come. It's going to be hard, and there are going to be moments that will leave you questioning your decision to be friends with them in the first place, but it does get better.

What we must realize is that this is okay. Sometimes we need to allow these mental Q&A sessions to play out organically. When you have the impetus to shut down a line of personal questioning due to fear of what you might find, I have found that this was often my anxiety talking for me. Deep breaths, quiet, and reflection all give the space to answer the questions we have for our past selves. Your wrestling with this—whether you do so through therapy, finding a new healthy routine, or talking with a loved one—is *good*. It means you're growing.

***

As I mentioned earlier in the chapter, my dedication to performing and the personal hardships that came with it hurt my academic life. I failed my biology course over a correct suspicion of academic dishonesty. I skipped class routinely and skipped most mandatory weekly discussion sessions in which we were to collect our small group of classmates' signatures to show we had attended. I took it upon myself to forge those signatures for several weeks. My professor could immediately see through my forgery as if holding up a fake bill of cash to the light, revealing a watermark. He decided to fail me rather than seek any harsher penalty; I am still grateful to him for that. To make matters worse, this was my second failed course of that year. I failed Italian 201 the prior semester due to my missing classes and overall inability to deal with any sort of work outside of performing. In my entire academic career up to this point, I had never received below a C grade. Suddenly, I had failed two courses.

This latest failure of biology shook me to my foundation and marked a watershed moment of my life. I will never forget returning to my apartment, closing my bedroom door, and beginning to weep as I called my mom to tell her. "This is rock bottom, Chris," she said.

She was right, but this did not help either. I was beyond just depressed. I was becoming despondent. I see this incident now as a cry for help that I was unable to explicitly give out loud. I also see how I capitulated to the bullying around me. It was on that day that I gave myself a lesson in resiliency by cleaning up the mess I'd made. Within an hour, I was enrolled in a make-up biology course slated for that coming summer. It was pass/fail, and I would have to find an apartment to stay on campus for a little bit longer. Given one more hour, I found another studio-sized apartment in the same complex.

That attitude of working my way out was contagious. Following my successful pass in summer biology, I spent the rest of that summer at home working out regularly, losing weight incrementally, and prepping for my coming internship. I built a force of positive momentum through working on myself.

My family would be traveling to England that summer, and it was supposed to be a celebratory vacation for me to also join. I would not be able to, however, as my biology course would fall smack dab in the middle of the trip. This added insult to injury, but it was another lesson that my actions do have very real consequences. With my family on another continent, I was alone, and found myself traveling to dark places as I sat by myself in my studio apartment night after night.

Instead of free falling into an even worse and more depressed and despondent state than before, I dug my heels in deeper at night. After finishing my homework from the day and doing any research for my upcoming internship, my attention would turn to the internet. Movies were slated to come out that summer that I was excited for, including *X-Men: Days of Future Past* and Marvel's *Guardians of the Galaxy*. I saw *X-Men* while living alone in Milwaukee and was enthralled.

I turned to movies and TV for inspiration many times during the following weeks. As an ardent fan of Henry Cavill's portrayal of Superman in 2013's *Man of Steel*, I watched and re-watched that. What I discovered was that the film's darker, more serious approach resonated deeply with me. In the movie, Superman is an alien who lives as an outsider and nomad throughout his young adult life. He is often alone and would need to stick up for himself while suppressing his superpowers. The scene where he takes his first flight choked me up upon my re-watch; it is a beautiful scene that showcases Clark Kent for the first time embracing his uniqueness and powers by flying. He is not in control of his flight path because it's his first time, but the montage shows him continuing to work out the kinks by simply continuing to fly.[52]

Then it dawned on me: I was attempting to fly in my own way.

That summer, I continued to work tirelessly to lose weight before beginning my internship. I jumped rope for the first time ever, I ran, and I did as many push-ups as I could muster (which was about ten at a time before giving out mentally and physically). The more I worked physically, the more I thought—wrongly—that I would earn an eating treat.

---

52 *Man of Steel*, directed by Zach Snyder (2005; Burbank, CA: Warner Bros. Pictures, 2013), Blu-ray Disc.

Food was always my Achilles heel. My routine of eating pizzas and cinnamon sticks regularly placed me into a hole that was deeper than I knew. My eating and drinking habits were horrific, and something that I cannot begin to comprehend now. The summer before my senior year at Marquette saw me regularly driving up to the new Starbucks drive through just around the corner from my house. Order a black coffee or even a coffee with "just" cream and sugar? *Absolutely* not! Why do that when white chocolate mochas and cinnamon dolce lattes were so readily available? Between each of these delicious-yet-calorically-dense drinks, Starbucks had my family's money lining their pockets at least three-to-four days per week that summer. This was the summer before beginning my transformation and the one in which I dug myself into a deeper hole than I was already in following the end of my junior year.

I became utterly complacent during this time of my life and often turned to food to achieve a high. I was a successful collegiate performer during my junior year, and I somehow believed that this—coupled with the lie I told myself that gaining weight would actually *help* me as a comedic performer—was already paving the way to professional success. Deep down I knew that nothing I did in college mattered in the professional world of theater, film, and TV save for the valuable personal experience gained through having not only been in productions, but a lead in productions. My own complacency was often fueled by those with whom I surrounded myself. This would continue, albeit in a professional setting with those who I expected to act as professionals.

***

Our orientation week to begin my acting internship at the Milwaukee Repertory Theater was filled with working ten-hour days in and out of meetings and preparing for the first show's read-through. I was one of two interns selected for a speaking role in the show, so I would have a seat at the table. I was thrilled, and the work was invigorating.

Part of our first week's itinerary was a one-on-one with the casting director, who had always been nice enough to me. I met him following a showcase done through Marquette. He introduced himself to me after the show and told me that I should apply for the theater's internship. We forged a bond over the summer while he was casting for a couple of the upcoming shows.

My excitement was palpable going into our one-on-one meeting because I had learned from other interns that we would talk about my "type," a term in the entertainment industry that refers to the roles for which one is best suited. I grew up as a huge TV and film fan and had come to familiarize myself with a great deal of men whom I aspired to emulate career-wise and personally.

One of these men was Hugh Jackman. The X-Men were some of my favorite comic book characters. Wolverine, the main anti-hero of the group, was in the running for my all-time favorite. It was amazing to watch Hugh Jackman conveying the ethos of Wolverine so effortlessly. I began to research him and his personal background and found that, on the surface, we seemed similar. My singing voice sounded like his, he played roles similar to those that I played in college, he performed both comedy and drama adeptly, and more than anything, he was not a cutthroat type of person. My dad had mentioned our similarities to me over the summer, and I took this as a sure sign.

Hugh Jackman was once told by a casting director that he was "too nice" to make a career in performing. This remained in the back of my mind as I sat down with my casting director because I was often told this too. Our discussion began cordially, and eventually, we segued into my "type." He volunteered his opinion, and amid this, I worked up the courage to add my own:

"What about Hugh Jackman?" I said. "My dad said it was a possibility, so I take it with kind of a grain of salt, but still, I think there could be something there…"

The casting director paused. He slightly leaned back in his chair, the pen suddenly emerging from his mouth, which was slightly agape.

"Well… maybe…" he began. "But Hugh Jackman is, obviously, more…" He searched for the right word for a couple of seconds. "He's just more… *toned*."

I sat back, slightly shocked, but mostly numb. It was clear to me that he was observing my weight and reacting to how far off base he felt I was. I had been called a "fat ass" plenty throughout grade school, junior high, high school, and even college. It was the first time in my then extremely young professional life that I had been called the same in so many words and in a supposedly professional setting.

Now, it wasn't quite *what* he said because nothing he had said was untrue. Hugh Jackman *was* more buff and toned than I was at the time—a mere six months into my journey of bettering my health and wellness and still sitting closer to three hundred pounds than two hundred. My confidence was brittle. It broke from his tone and utter dismissal of me. I had been routinely dismissed by performing colleagues at Marquette who were too insecure to keep their own brokenness to themselves, but this, from a man who was my direct superior and who I would be working alongside for the next nine months, was extremely hard for me to swallow. I was firmly grounded back to reality: my progress, while sizable in my eyes, was not so in the eyes of others. My willpower took a dive that day. I went home, had a bagel with peanut butter and watched Netflix to "soothe" my brokenness.

The next day, however, I woke up, which I saw as a victory in and of itself. I did not disappear from feeling so small, and that helped me climb out of bed. Though I was more anxious than ever to walk to the bathroom to glance at that "soft" figure, when I arrived at the mirror, I was proud. I was proud that I *had* begun a journey to bettering myself, even if I was not where I wanted to be.

That morning, I found *Man of Steel* online again and pressed play. Soon after beginning the film, I stopped it—I wanted to work out. Even if I did not look like Henry Cavill did in *Man of Steel*, it was a goal of mine to try not only because of my yearning for more self-confidence but also because of the surefire health benefit to come with it. I was tired of aching all over for no apparent reason. I wanted to be toned physically, yes, but more so emotionally and spiritually.

That day has stayed with me as the first time I can remember consciously choosing to *fight*. I was fighting my own self-doubt and my negative self-talk, which were absolutely encouraged by those who openly doubted me and did not support me, but these people were not whom I was consciously fighting against. I fought against myself and my then-derisive mindset. In doing so, I made myself accountable to somebody for the first time in years: myself.

***

The friction that came along with holding myself accountable brought about an immense amount of anxiety. I was not used to living in the real world because my responsibility had appeared to leave me. There was no accountability to what I ate or how I exercised, and I had enormous trust issues coming out of Marquette due to the people I met and the isolation I found. I had difficulty maintaining to what and whom to be responsible. It sucked most days. It was especially difficult at the beginning of the journey when I even had trust issues with myself after my downward spiral at Marquette. There are still days where the "easier" path can be seductive, but this does not always have to be the case.

Working on yourself and holding yourself accountable means that you are competitive with nobody but *you*. This removes the consideration of others and the sometimes gripping temptation to compare yourself with their journeys. By only focusing on you, your life, and your priorities, life is made simpler. In my experience, your love, care, and consideration for others only deepens because of how involved you can become by focusing on improving your own world and working from the inside out.

This was not a reality I discovered until years into my journey. The natural atmosphere was often for peers to compare themselves to other peers, and this was where passive aggression and cattiness reared their hideous heads. Many tore others down to try and raise themselves up. The phrase that stuck with me as a summation of my time while performing is an age-old adage derived from famed playwright Christopher Marlowe's sixteenth century play *Dr. Faustus*: "Misery loves company."[53] I allowed myself to become bogged down in considering what others thought about me and what was said about me when I wasn't around. I became paranoid while not knowing who I could trust.

Despite this paranoia, fear, depression, and anxiety I experienced, there remained one constant. I still showed up. I was paralyzed by fear and depression during my time at college. I could not move some days and chose to stay in bed rather than venture out to class. This was a specific sensation wherein I gave over complete control of my mind, body, and spirit to the demons that tormented me. My chemical imbalance in my own brain certainly did not help, but there was enough of me there to realize that what I was doing was wrong.

While I was placed in a state of mind that affected my decision making, I was often driven into deeper depression when

---

53 *The London Series of English Classics: Doctor Faustus,* not. by Wilhelm Wagner (London, England: Longmans, Green, and Co., 1918), Scene V, line 43.

knowing, deep down, that my actions were the wrong ones thanks to my lifelong innate guilty conscious. Having to go for a workout when feeling an intense amount of shame, guilt, and awfulness about myself pounded into me by my depression brought about a whole new meaning to the word "challenge."

Looking back, I now see these as challenges to my own willpower. Willpower challenges such as these are tests for our souls in times of great adversity. Just thinking about my experiences with Mike and the casting director in Milwaukee were once triggers for severe anxiety attacks. They would bring about a sense of dread that felt insurmountable. Even while working out, these thoughts began to permeate my brain at the first sign of fatigue and would pummel me into submission more often than not. Now these same thoughts have become fuel to run my body's willpower. Challenges that test our character and minds to the utmost are true "willpower tests." Know that, as with any test, you are more than capable of passing with flying colors worthy of Superman.

CHAPTER 8

Movement & Finding Your Why

You're huffing. You're puffing. Your heart rate speeds rapidly. Beads of sweat begin streaming with consistency down your forehead as it sleds over your nose and onto the pavement. You begin feeling like you're going to blow yourself over from your breaths that seem to come from deep within your soul.

This is the picture of vigorous exercise for people who run the gamut between in shape and out of shape. You may run a couple times per week, make it to the gym every other day, or even go frequently but tried a much more intense regimen than you are used to. Your heart rate climbs steadily, you begin sweating more and more as time goes on, and your fight or flight reflex is eventually triggered after crossing a personal intensity threshold.

This is the physiological response to exercise.

This is also the physiological response to stress.

When we exercise, we put our body through a ringer of stressful situations. No matter what form our exercise takes, all of our bodies react by creating micro-tears in our muscles. These inconceivably tiny tears are part of that soreness that often comes after exercising; however, just as our body slightly tears through the musculature, it also recovers in an amazing way: it adapts to the stress that caused those tears and heals our muscles in a way that makes us more capable of handling that load.

So if you attempted a bench press of 135 pounds as your personal best, your body might feel sore in the time immediately following, but you have just made your chest more likely to be able to handle that load when you step up to try again in a few days. This micro-tear healing process in the muscles is known scientifically as hypertrophy. [54] Through the hypertrophy process, humans become stronger.

Hypertrophy provides a microcosm of what introducing more stress over time does to not only our bodies but also our minds.

***

As people, we were designed to move. Our earliest ancestors were hunter-gatherers, so physical activity was ingrained into their everyday routines as a necessity to survive. As time has gone on, while an inherent physicality has remained—some walking, some standing, some overall movement in the everyday lives of the most sedentary—it is but a fraction

---

54   *Merriam-Webster*, s.v. "hypertrophy (n.)," accessed January 2, 2020.

of what it once was. New technology, desk-bound jobs, and attitudes towards exercise are but a few of the reasons why people's desire to move has dwindled.

I have often found myself in the camp of not wanting to move. Even now, there are plenty of days where my desire to get up and train feels near non-existent. You don't get to near three hundred unhealthy pounds twice in life without there being plenty of avoidance-of-exercise-at-all-costs entrenched in the mind.

What is ironic about this is that during the second period of my life where I gained a massive amount of weight, I was moving plenty every day. As any student who attended a college with a large enough campus can attest, walking to and from class can entail miles of consistent moving. As a freshman at Indiana, my round trip to a single class and back to my dorm was often at least two miles. At Marquette, while the school was smaller and the campus more accessible, I lived off-campus my junior and senior years in an apartment five blocks from the beginnings of campus. I can guess now that my daily walking was anywhere between three to six miles per day.

This is all to say a couple of things. First, sometimes, we need to acknowledge movement *whenever* it happens, and not just when we feel exhausted or sweaty. Walking may not "sound" like exercise, but it is the most underrated form of it that there is, in my opinion. Studies have shown it to decrease aggression and hostility.[55] Walking through greenery and

---

55   Meghan Rabbitt, "11 Biggest Benefits of Walking to Improve Your Health, According to Doctors," Prevention, accessed January 5, 2020.

natural settings have proven to aid with symptoms of depression and help improve memory.[56] Moving our bodies actively engages our muscles, causing better blood flow throughout, and our brain is one of the muscles that benefits from this.

The second major takeaway from my own story is that, while movement is integral to improving our moods and bettering our overall health, it cannot be solely relied upon. Sleep is yet another integral part of maintaining a healthy lifestyle, as this is the stage of each day that our bodies recover most. The deep sleep stage specifically plays an integral role in restoring our physical health. When you wake up feeling refreshed, you most likely had a night full of productive deep sleep. The light sleep and REM cycle stages are also integral; while lightly sleeping, we relax our bodies, and within the REM cycle, we maintain learned information and are restored mentally. What's better news is that if you are hugely productive during the day, it follows that you should be much more likely to need sleep, and so falling asleep is easier.[57]

Another key to maintaining a healthy lifestyle is eating and drinking healthily. This sounds obvious. but for many, it is not.

You can be hugely active in going to the gym for hours a day, running miles upon miles, or being a prolific walker; if your

---

56 "Interacting with nature improves cognition and affect for individuals with depression," *Journal of Affective Disorders* 140, issue 3 (November 2012): 300-305.

57 "Brain Basics: Understanding Sleep," Patient & Caregiver Information, National Institute of Neurological Disorders and Stroke, accessed January 2, 2020.

diet is not in order, however, there will be very little physical and mental results. Our diets—which I am defining here simply as what we choose to eat and drink consistently each day—often play the defining role in shaping our outlooks on life.

While I was a college student, I struggled mightily with sleep and eating. Had I attacked both with some semblance of discipline, I would have stayed relatively healthy throughout college purely because of how much walking I was doing. But I didn't, and the results spoke for themselves: I was complacent, insecure, out of shape mentally and physically, and ultimately disoriented most of the time. As time went on, it took me twice or three times as long to retain information as it did when I was training regularly and eating healthily in the time just before. My interest in activities that once brought me joy dwindled, and my depression and anxiety took over full time.

What I found once I started to pull all three of these factors—sleep, eating, and moving—to work together was that, while it hurt and was miserable at the beginning, it slowly began to seem *worth* it. Even now, there are plenty of days where I don't *want* to go train or have broccoli as a side with dinner but do crave a whole plate of French toast cake balls.

It is the frequency with which I do indulge that has changed and the mindfulness with which I now do so. It is now a small fraction of the amount of times I did before. Eat the cake, pizza, cupcakes, and/or cake balls—just know you still have a day of work ahead tomorrow. When you *live* healthily, each day presents more work to do on yourself. This is a good thing: once you have lived this way long enough, it will become as natural as breathing. You won't be able to imagine your prior life where you did *not* live this way.

As you truly live out the ideal *healthy* life, *happiness* will inevitably insert itself as the natural corollary.

This all sounds so good, I know. I also know that if it was easy to live your life healthily and with your best interest at heart first, everybody would do it. It is hard as hell. You must possess a true desire to see each day as an opportunity to become better. This needs to be especially true on the days where you feel your worst because your fatigue or poor mood won't change anything. **Full disclosure, you should absolutely rest if you would be risking injury or becoming sicker by doing anything else.**

It's the days where you don't *feel* like moving, or getting out of bed when your alarm goes off at five a.m., or adhering to your diet, or skipping out on a work project that are the problem. Not *feeling* like it is not good enough. I know this from a full past of personal experience, including my present day. To get through this, I have often reassured myself that fatigue and exhaustion are inevitable. As those are inevitable, so too is my dedication to myself. This how I've learned to put the principle of discipline in action.

When I truly feel low and in a darker mood, I start by moving. I put my body in motion before I would ever allow myself to acknowledge that I was "ready" to be. The journey to losing one hundred pounds, putting that weight and then some back on, and losing one hundred more pounds is littered with its share of gut punches from life. You will get knocked down plenty. As your commitment to yourself grows, however, these falls won't be catastrophic. They will prove the opposite. Some, like David Goggins, learned to cherish the fall because of the opportunity to fight his way back up again.

***

Everybody's journey is different. Different methods of exercise will affect everyone uniquely. Healthy eating and drinking habits and sleep schedules are also deeply personal. What is universal, however, are the values that go into seeing each of these commitments through. There is no better illustration of this idea than the late John Wooden's *Pyramid of Success*.[58]

John Wooden is arguably the most famous college basketball coach in the history of the sport. As the head coach of the UCLA Bruins men's basketball team from 1948 through 1976, his record of achievements is staggering (ten national championships in a twelve year period between 1964-1975, including seven in a row, and an eighty-eight game winning streak at one point). Part of what made him so successful was his belief in nurturing fully formed young men. He believed in each player graduating with a degree and leaving as a well-rounded human being.[59]

He devised the pyramid of success over a fourteen-year period, culminating in 1948 when he took the head coaching position at UCLA. He put as the pyramid's cornerstones

---

[58] "About the Pyramid of Success," About Coach, The Wooden Effect, accessed January 3, 2020.
[59] "About Coach," The Wooden Effect, accessed January 3, 2020.

"industriousness" and "enthusiasm." Industriousness' definition reads, "There is no substitution for work. Worthwhile results come from hard work and careful planning." He defined enthusiasm as "brushes off on those with whom you come in contact. You must truly enjoy what you are doing."[60]

At the pyramid's peak, he placed "competitive greatness." He described this poetically: "Be at your best when your best is needed[...]The hard battle inspires and motivates a great competitor to dig deep inside." Within the external space between each tier, he placed the factors needed to achieve each higher level. To reach competitive greatness, he posited that one needed "integrity" ("purity of intention") and "fight" ("determined effort"). He wrote, spoke, and taught about this pyramid until his death in 2010.[61]

Coach Wooden's success pyramid dictates just how much value and intention behind what it is we choose to do each day foretells the success of each endeavor. As a man who lived his own pyramid, he showcased the effectiveness of the journey from the very bottom to achieving competitive greatness. Everything in life is not a competition; however, I believe possessing a healthy competitiveness gives your psyche an edge as you work. Contrary to popular belief in a culture that often encourages a cutthroat approach towards others, the competitions do not need to involve anybody outside of yourself.

I attribute a sizable amount of my maintaining and continuing to improve in all aspects of my life due to my

---

60 Kristin Edelhauser, "John Wooden's Pyramid Still Standing," Entrepreneur, accessed January 3, 2020.
61 "About the Pyramid of Success," The Wooden Effect.

competitiveness with myself. This voice, which I ironically call "Coach," is ever present within my own psyche. The voice keeps me honest, accountable, and tells me when I may be slacking. I developed this voice out of necessity. My nature as an introvert coupled with the little support I had while undertaking my journey to turning my life around created Coach organically. What's wonderful is that I know I'm not alone in having this voice.

When I call myself out, I often don't like hearing it because it means I was not tapping into the *best* that I have to offer. But after that initial wave of regret, my mind turns to what I need to do to remedy whatever the situation might be. As you work your way along in your own journey and you become more and more self-confident, your self-talk will improve. As your self-talk improves, so too will your view of calling yourself out. You will be able to see that you are doing it *because* you care about you, your health, and the happiness of everybody in your life.

You will welcome these challenges described by Coach Wooden as you find your voice and the values behind living healthily. Once these values become part of your lifestyle—which happens through showing up *every* day, even when you don't feel like it—you will achieve consistency, and your lifestyle will achieve staying power. With discipline comes the ability to have principles.

Maybe you make it a principle to study every day for an upcoming exam for at least one hour or until you have a firm understanding of the concept. You have promised yourself that you will. These promises can only become principles, and vice versa, through regular practice and regular internal work on your emotional state.

Ultimately, what Coach Wooden's values do is cut through the surface and bring these changes to a deeply personal place. To eat, sleep, drink, and move with healthy consistency, and to fully define the values (like integrity and character) to which you will adhere, you will need your *why*, as in "Why am I doing this?"

There will be moments and days—maybe even weeks or months—where your mind will be imploring you to tell it *why* you are choosing the harder path. If there is no healthy, personal answer to that seemingly simple question, more often than not, our brain will win. It will badger you into submission as soon as you're confronted with that difficulty. What becomes integral, in my experience, is the ability to be able to stare it down with aplomb and repeat your mantra, or your reasons for *why*.

These are reasons that only you ever must know. Your "why" should cut to your core and possess the ready ability to repel that mental reaction of repeatedly questioning us while experiencing adversity. Again, having an answer to "Why?" might sound simple. Fortunately, it is anything but. The meaningful work you put into yourself in finding your core reason(s) for changing your life will mean that the turnaround will be long-lasting and meaningful.

Some people find their answers outside of themselves. Their "why" is because if they don't get up early every day and train at the gym before working their two jobs, their family won't have food to eat at the end of each month. Their "why" exists to fulfill the human desires of others. Some find their "why" within themselves—their internal competitiveness is so great that they must find new ways to better each achievement. Or there is a personal or health scare that ignites change to optimize personal health. In my case, my initial "why" was that I needed to lose weight to stave off serious and potentially lethal health conditions from being obese.

The values Coach Wooden outlined in his pyramid can help with identifying what you might need to improve on or see through to fully be honest with yourself, slice to your core, and ultimately, deal with any emotional scar tissue to honestly define your "why."

READER PROMPT
- Find a ten-minute window in your day for quiet time. This should be time made for only you in your room, office, family room, etc.
- Write down a list of at least five reasons *why* your desire to change or transform your life exists.
    - Write down at least five past accomplishments that you are proud of under these.
- Carry this list with you. When you find yourself in an adverse or stressful circumstance, you can know that your list of "whys" and accomplishments are tangibly with you.

CHAPTER 9

Vulnerability & Happiness

To discover your truest self, you must confront your demons and put them in their rightful place: an 8x8 mental jail cell that only you have access to. As has been mentioned, this must be done in the way that suits you best, as there is no single linear path to getting better.

Another common trait amongst successful people I have the great fortune to know, have studied, and have grown into myself is the idea of harnessing our internal darkness for good. Once again, each individual person has their own individual way of doing this, which means that there is no objectively right or wrong way of coping.

Famous comedians often create jokes around the most personal and touchy topics one could reach for. These are often borne out of personal experience. A common phrase in the world of comedy is that there is great truth and humanity in the best comedic bits.

I learned this first hand while a student of comedy in The Second City Chicago's famed conservatory and iO Chicago's summer intensive program. Both focus primarily on improvisational comedy and how it lives as a singular art form. Perhaps the most famous tenet of improv. comedy is the principle of "Yes, and…" When one employs this foundational belief of improvisation, you not only agree to your scene partner's idea but also add your own flavor to it.

For example, my scene partner might enter and initiate a scene by saying, "Hark! There be a castle!" The "wrong" way to respond would be by asserting, "That's not a castle! It's a spaceship!" The "right" way would be to respond by agreeing to the established environment and adding to it, so my response might be, "Aye! There is a castle! And it has the tiniest moat I have ever seen as its defense!"

Employing this while performing takes a great deal of trust, commitment, and ultimately, vulnerability. To submit to trusting and committing fully to the scene, one must find their inner vulnerability and humanity to not only agree and add to what's been established but also to do so in a believable way.

What is so amazing about the principles of successful improvisational comedy is that they apply to each facet of living a productive life. Every person is capable of improvising on stage; we do it every day in every conversation we have as is. Submitting to vulnerability to tell the truth, whether it be on stage or in my everyday life, has greatly aided in my journey in discovering and pushing long past any perceived limits and embracing the discomfort that often comes in times of great adversity.

***

From my experience, being vulnerable is associated with negativity from the jump. It is not associated with overtly positive feelings; in fact, the opposite is true.

The word itself is derived from the Latin noun *vulnus,* which means "wound." This progressed to the Latin verb *vulnerare,* or "to wound." In the early seventeenth century, the Late Latin adjective *vulnerabilis* emerged, and this meant "vulnerable." As we can see from this syntactical history, the very roots of the word vulnerable evoke the idea of damaging oneself or others.[62]

This association with harm is consistent with Merriam-Webster's 2021 definition of vulnerable, which reads, "Capable of being physically or emotionally wounded; open to attack or damage."[63] It makes sense, then, that we are often told to be careful when being vulnerable. Trust if you must and always be careful is the prevailing notion one learns as one matures and grows. This is not untrue. In adulthood, it's practical to adhere to this code; the animalistic evolutionary nature to protect ourselves and those we love is perhaps our strongest instinct. We absolutely need to protect and ensure the health and happiness of ourselves and others we love.

---

62   *Merriam-Webster,* s.v. "vulnerable (n.)," accessed February 12, 2021.
63   Ibid.

When we begin to own ourselves, our stories, and who *we* are as people, however, vulnerability becomes second nature. It is not always seen as the vulnerability that involves wounding. Pulling the curtain back and allowing others to see who you genuinely are is usually appreciated by those with whom you share. So why is there this stigma against the word vulnerable and the very act of being vulnerable itself?

Well, on the surface, I believe some of it has to do with societal roles every gender has been assigned throughout the course of history. Men are expected to be the stoic workers who provide and women are expected to be the emotional caretakers of the home, and this shuts both sides completely out of the vulnerable conversation. Men should not be viewed as vulnerable for fear of being known as weak, and women can be *too* vulnerable and emotional, according to this belief system. So, neither side gets the ability to be positively vulnerable.

What this "old fashioned world" also doesn't account for is the welcome gray area in how a growing population of people choose to identify by gender. Non-binary, transgender, agender: these are all terms that within the past ten to fifteen years have become more and more prevalent due to peoples' openness to being vulnerable and sharing their truths. So, what is their role in society? What do they do? This evolving understanding of gender is yet another way, in my opinion, that this age-old belief in the man as stoic and the woman as overly-emotional is just that: ages old.

And I believe that, more deeply, the root of vulnerability's stigma comes from a lack of belief in ourselves and inner joy.

***

For those who would identify as self-confident, consider how often you care about other people's opinions about you and your character. Whether these opinions be good or bad, do you invest deep emotional energy into considering them? I would posit that, for the most self-confident among us, there would be little to no investment precisely due to the nature of self-confidence. Self-confidence implies you draw from your own internal well, with maybe a minuscule amount of confidence being gained from external sources, like one's job or school performance. So external opinions regarding your state of being would, more than likely, minimally register.

For those who identified as self-confident but took issue with the question above, I would challenge you to take a harder look at yourself internally. Are you really as *self-confident* as you believe? The line between cocky and self-destructive is thin, meaning those who are cocky might have had the same reaction and answer as those who honestly identify with having little self-confidence. If you took issue with the question, I would also venture to guess that being vulnerable might be difficult for you, as it might be viewed as a weakness or even wholly unnecessary.

When we possess a confidence and belief in ourselves, vulnerability—while absolutely still taking a measure of courage and acknowledgment of the uncertainty of the outcome—becomes much less scary and much more of an opportunity. When we possess a skin that is armored by our minds rather than an outer layer of armor protecting an otherwise vulnerable skin, I believe we become increasingly less susceptible to the potential negative outcomes from being vulnerable.

Here again I draw from my vast personal experience. At the time of my writing this book, I have only recently become more comfortable with being vulnerable with loved ones, casual acquaintances, and perfect strangers alike. My life experience as a professional performer dictated that vulnerability was at the fore of my mind. To convincingly and realistically portray the arc of a character, even if it was in a two-minute comedic sketch, there had to be vulnerability from within myself to fully empathize with the character being portrayed. Because I wasn't classically trained in performance, I didn't know how to invest so emotionally in a character for a few hours of rehearsal or a show before turning those emotions off as I left the theater. This confusion left me internally scattered as I often found myself trying to dig myself out of dark emotional rabbit holes.

This is to say that where I went off the rails was not knowing exactly *how* vulnerability and its potentially negative consequences could be used against me. I walked around emotionally vulnerable most of my waking life. I didn't know how to respond when somebody did not reciprocate my own show of vulnerability or had a negative reaction. I was not self-confident and did not have the tools to cope with being pushed to the side. I was impressionable and extremely sensitive, with no mind-powered armor on my skin to speak of.

What has changed is how I have come to see being vulnerable in a brand new light. It is a show of strength of character and personality when one chooses to be vulnerable. I have come to believe that simply being true to who you are can leave you vulnerable. But here is the catch: those who are true to who they are and happy with that tend to not *feel* vulnerable, even if they are being vulnerable. Here, words can matter. Just as stress can be harnessed for good, so too can vulnerability. Both have their roots in negativity, but both don't always have to be inherently negative.

Of course, we aren't robots. We're human and made up of a complex system of thoughts and emotions that means there will always be *some* level of uncertainty or risk by being vulnerable, even for the most self-assured and happy among us, but we can mitigate the anxiety surrounding this uncertainty by being courageous and vulnerable in all facets of our life by owning ourselves. While my journey is personal to me, I have found that the idea of true happiness and self-confidence being present helps with being vulnerable.

Happiness is within our grasp if we so choose. The good news is that there is some scientific and philosophical merit to this belief.

***

The belief and hypothesis that humans can manifest happiness has a rich history rooted in science, philosophy, and psychology. Famous psychologist and philosopher William James, who practiced during the nineteenth century, had a prominent theory on happiness. After obtaining his M.D., he suffered from serious depression brought on by his intensive scientific studies. He described his depression as a "crisis of meaning." He came out of this deep depressive state soon after reading an essay by famed philosopher Charles Renouvier. It was at this moment that he decided that free will, will power, and conviction in personal beliefs were not illusions—these were reality, so long as he chose to believe that they were. "My first act of free will will be to believe in free will," he wrote in his diary.[64]

In his 1890 book *Principles of Psychology*, he goes to greater lengths to detail the phenomenon of free will and how it affects our choosing happiness. He argues that voluntary movements are secondary and not primary functions of human life. We are spectators surprised by our primary actions; however, after each movement is done once, it's in our memory, and we can thusly choose it whenever we want. Secondarily, he says that happiness requires an "as if" mindset. We must live as if our deeper meaning exists within the world, even if we have no concrete evidence of that.[65] James famously wrote, "Believe that life is worth living, and your very belief will help create the fact."[66]

James also posited that those who experience adversity or deep depressions are more prone to finding more lasting, meaningful happiness. Those who undergo a crisis of meaning, as James called it, are also more prone to wanting to discover *why* they feel how they do. This inevitably leads to

---

64 *The Thought and Character of William James* (Nashville, TN: Vanderbilt University Press, 1996), 323.
65 *The Principles of Psychology, Vol. 2, Revised Ed.* (Garden City, New York: Dover Publications, 2012), chap. 26, Kindle.
66 *Pragmatism and Other Writings* (New York: Penguin Classics, 2000), 240, Kindle.

discovering that the very act of seeking to understand is positive, which undercuts the negativity felt during a depression. Those who undergo this transformation are "Second Born," James said, and often see life more joyfully and more meaningfully than others who never reach their nadir.[67]

James' writings on the meaning of life and human happiness can serve as an undercurrent for bringing more positivity into your life or the lives of your loved ones. It's a simple and incredible thought to posit that deep, profound happiness is perpetually within our grasps. All we must do is make the choice.

An example I love to use from my own life is reading. Growing up, I did not consider myself a "reader." I *always* preferred to watch stories being told through film and TV over sitting down with a good book and reading. My movie collection grew exponentially over the years, and I became a DVD rental service within my dorms in college. If friends wanted to borrow a movie, they could sign it out and make sure to have it back within a couple days.

I loved and still love movies and TV. A couple of years ago, however, I decided to give reading a try as I was yearning to find a new hobby. Living in Chicago afforded ample opportunity to visit libraries. I got my library card after moving downtown in 2018 and began my journey. It took greasing my intellectual wheels to get going, but once I did, I never looked back. I still haven't. I've read more books in the three

---

67 *The Varieties of Religious Experience: A Study in Human Nature* (London: Longmans, Green, and Co., 1851), 157, eBook.

years after that than I did in my entire life leading up to that. And now I'm a "reader."

I'm only a reader because I've actively chosen to be one. I was vulnerable with myself to acknowledge that, growing up, I wasn't open to being one. The *truth* is, I was—and we all are—capable of becoming a reader, but do we all indulge in our ability to read? Those who do are known as readers or "bookworms." Those who do not are not.

This same principle applies to happiness, especially as seen through the lens of William James. At some point within our earliest years, we have our first happy moment. That's our primary action. Whether we consciously remember exactly what it was or not, it's in our bodies and ready to be used again as a secondary action. So we create the environment for ourselves to find happiness in life. Depression, adversity, and hardship will inevitably hit, but we've given ourselves the gift of having the ability to have a happy, joyful outlook on life even through these hard moments.

We have a *choice* to see life as dark and meaningless, just as we have a choice to indulge in the beauty and wonder it provides. This doesn't mean it's going to be easy. Nor should this *ever* be used to prove to somebody with a mental illness that they can just "get over it." **It is never that simple with mental illness. And, once again, if you feel you are experiencing mental illness, please seek help. If you feel you know somebody who might be, check in on them; these gestures of love go a long way.** I have only come to this point of acknowledging the merit of William James *because* I have treated my own mental illness first.

Dealing with your inner demons takes courage, and once again, *vulnerability*. Happiness will be waiting patiently for you on the other side.

CHAPTER 10

So Do It.

I leapt down the final three stairs of my family's home in Naperville, Illinois in a rush, sprinted across our kitchen to the key rack, and opened the adjacent garage door. It was September 2016, and I had moved back home to Chicago from Los Angeles after a near-exact one year living there. While pursuing performing in LA without an official college degree and six credits short, I was deeply unhappy. At the time, it seemed it was the city—too spread out, too busy, too much of a place for seemingly twenty-four hour socializing. As I prepared to move back, I did some research on degree requirements for an English major at Marquette University. To my surprise, I found they had changed to my benefit!

I began a correspondence with a member of Marquette's registrar's office which lasted two weeks. Then, I applied to graduate by the end of July at her recommendation and to meet the cut-off for August graduation. I moved back home to Chicago in early August; by the end of August, I was an official graduate of Marquette University with a bachelor's degree in English. It was a check off my mental list and an enormous weight off my entire back.

Up until that point, I felt I had failed myself, my parents, the rest of my family, and even close friends. I lived with a deep-seated self-shame. This was a feeling toward myself that I'd kept for years on end. My demeanor had changed into one that was pleasant on the surface and sometimes overly nice to compensate for my deep guilt around how my time at Marquette ended. Even while enjoying professional success as a performer, I began to look at myself as an imposter, undeserving of any accolade or career advancement. This feeling of inauthentic achievement due to luck is called imposter syndrome, and it's a debilitating sensation.[68]

Following my graduation, and despite the immense weight off my shoulders, I remained depressed and lonely. Many of the people I met while at Marquette had turned out to be not as genuinely interested in me as I had thought. I am sure many would tell you that I withdrew, and that is also true. I was a wounded person, and to heal, I removed myself from social situations. But in this case, I did not bring the pain wholly on myself; it came partially because of my harmful treatment at the hands of classmates.

As I've mentioned before, I have experienced bullying at every level of school I have attended—from preschool through my undergraduate career in college. Many of the insults remained the same: "fat ass," "bitch," and "pussy" were all staples for most tormentors. My size growing up was so much larger than my classmates that I literally stood out more than most. My shyness and soft-spoken nature did not help either.

---

68 *Merriam-Webster*, s.v. "impostor syndrome (n.)," accessed January 10, 2020.

I so desperately wanted to fit in that I chose friends who subverted my own dignity. I did so from grade school through college and even in the couple years following my graduation.

One example of the type of bullying I experienced as a kid came during a trip to the movies. It was 2004, I was thirteen, and the Steve Carell comedy vehicle *The 40-Year-Old Virgin* was just released. Cinemark strung a large, forty-foot high poster on its grandiose walls. As my "friend" and I strolled into the lobby, we talked about something unimportant to me. All that I can remember are his words to me after seeing the supersized poster. *"Hey, look!"* He laughed. *"That'll be you someday, just fatter and uglier."* I felt myself go emotionally numb simply to get through our time together.

It's a strange thing to actively choose to befriend somebody who subverts one's own dignity to seek approval and be liked. This sounds like an oxymoron of the highest order, but it happens all the time. I am sure that many of you reading can think of a time when being friends with somebody who was "cool" took priority over having self-respect. It happens throughout life. Even now, close friends talk about how they don't like being friendly with certain coworkers who do not return the courtesy but feel that it's necessary to further their careers. This approach is *wild* to truly consider. Politicking in the workplace is common, and the desire to fulfill the human need to connect often supersedes choosing our own personal dignity by not associating with those who put us and others down. Oftentimes, we cede control to those who put us down by choosing to play into their false narratives. Throughout my life, I have done this too many times to count.

Bullies gain control over those around them every day. Per 2020 data from StopBullying.gov, bullying in school affects as many as 33 percent of kids and young adults, and its effects can be varied and life long.[69] Those who directly experience bullying are more likely to experience depression, anxiety, and decreased academic performance. They are more likely to skip or miss school. Those who do the bullying are more likely to abuse drugs and alcohol, be abusive to romantic partners, and have criminal convictions. Even bystanders of bullying are not exempt from its toxicity; they have also been found to be more likely to experience depression, anxiety, and decreased academic performance.[70] In my case, I have experienced depression, anxiety, decreased academic performance, and a greater likelihood to mistrust others. Bullying has no winners.

To regain control of my life, I returned to my roots as an active person. Beginning in first grade with tee ball and lasting into the beginning part of my college life, I was always an active person interested in team sports. Throughout my soul searching, I came to find that simply remaining true to myself and who I have always been has played an immense role in turning around my life. "Simply" is a deceptive word here because of how complicated this process of self-discovery often is.

Here too lies an interesting and integral dichotomy: no matter what your perceived social standing or community is, there is no escape from bullies. As an athlete, I recognized

---

[69] "Effects of Bullying," Resources, StopBullying.gov, last modified July 21, 2020.

[70] "Effects of Bullying," Resources, StopBullying.gov, last modified July 21, 2020.

early on as a grade schooler that my makeup was different than that of many of my teammates. I did not have the proclivity to bully others or to even just give them a hard time. I knew that I would not appreciate it then, so I didn't do it to anybody else. This made me a target, even as a starter and high achiever on the many basketball, baseball, and football teams of which I was a part.

Everybody's journey is different. Not everybody needs to lose one hundred pounds. Not everybody needs to put themselves on a "diet" or compete athletically to feel personally validated or healthy. I have been fortunate to observe people who are comfortable in their own skin and who are not the stereotypical image of "healthy." This utter comfort with oneself becomes contagious to be around. Owning who *you* are and discovering strength to project from the inside out is the root. This ownership comes, by all accounts, from recognizing personal value and worth even in the face of bullying. Recognizing your personal individuality as your superpower is one way to begin.

People will always talk, nobody finds love and acceptance from everybody they meet, and bullying will always be part of the world. It's a harsh reality, but it's also a necessary one to acknowledge to take that next step. That next step is you finding it within yourself to tap into the inherent willpower and grit you possess. Your discovery of these innate powers will then go an immensely long way to finding the success you wish to achieve no matter what field you find work in or subject in school you study.

***

Dr. Angela Duckworth is one of the foremost scholars on grit and mental toughness. In a viral TED Talk from 2013, she cited her study of people in challenging environments. She and her research team attended West Point Military Academy to study and attempt to predict who might last in military training. She went to tough neighborhoods to study rookie teachers' effectiveness in relaying their messages. She even attended the National Spelling Bee to try and predict who would advance furthest in competition.[71]

"In all those very different contexts," she shared, "one characteristic emerged as a significant predictor of success." It wasn't social intelligence, attractiveness, or even I.Q. It was grit.[72]

She defined grit as "passion and perseverance for very long-term goals." She described it as "living life like it's a marathon, not a sprint."[73] This final image invoked is a helpful one. Life in pursuit of your goals will come with extreme highs and lows as any marathon runner could tell you. Sometimes, miles twenty through twenty-two feel like the hardest portion of the race—it's towards the end, and mentally, that many people begin giving more credence to voices that are actively encouraging quitting. This comes despite the fact there are only four to six more miles to go. Your mind has a way of playing to those insecurities and getting you to tap out early.

David Goggins has often stated that when most people choose to stop an arduous or challenging task, they are truly

---

[71] TED, "Grit: the power of passion and perseverance | Angela Lee Duckworth," May 9, 2013, video, 6:12.
[72] Ibid.
[73] Ibid.

only 40 percent done. He calls it his "40 Percent Rule." When you think you're done and like you have nothing left to give, you're only about 40 percent *truly* done.[74]

I understand that this sounds vague, but it isn't. While this can't be empirically measured using science to identify one's *exact* 40 percent, the point David Goggins has made repeatedly through the definition of this rule is this: *you have so much left to give when you think that you don't.* This is precisely where the mind having a tactical advantage comes back into play. The mind's effort to play on your insecurities and fears often sets the cap at 40 percent. This is another re-invocation of his idea that we have governors, like the ones found within cars, inherently placed within our minds to keep us at a comfortable speed. It is only when we remove this mental mechanism that we begin to discover the other 60 percent untapped potential.

Goggins has often said that this "cap"—when we often feel we are finished—comes from the active journey to find comfort. People prefer ease over struggle. The mind, when put in a stressful situation, kicks your comfort voice into overdrive. "You can be done now," it will shout.[75] As the survivor of two Navy SEAL "Hell Weeks" in one year and graduating US Army Ranger School as the Enlisted Honor Man, David's knowledge comes from intimate personal experience.[76]

---

74   David Goggins, *Can't Hurt Me: Master Your Mind and Defy the Odds* (Austin, Texas: Lioncrest Publishing, 2018), 210-213.
75   "There is Only One David Goggins," About, DavidGoggins.com, accessed January 12, 2020.
76   "Years of Athletic Achievement," Achievements, DavidGoggins.com, accessed January 12, 2020.

When I began running at nearly three hundred pounds after having finished my time at Marquette as a full-time student, my body and mind screamed in pain and in search for comfort. I will never forget one of my first runs. I began by running on Marquette's campus while enrolled in summer biology following the second semester of my would-be senior year. I attempted to run five blocks down the road, around the rec center's large plot of land, and back up in eighty degree weather at sunset. This was about one mile in total. As I reached the rec center, I stopped—my lungs felt on the verge of explosion as my throat burned from desperately attempting to breathe. It felt as if I was submerged in a tub of water, trying to climb out, and slipping back in every time I tried to escape.

Despite that pain, I finished. I did not run the entire course, but I *did* it. Though I didn't realize it at the time, I had created momentum for myself into the next day, which would surely find me in pain. Spoiler alert—it did. But over time, the pain became a reminder to myself that I had followed through on a promise to myself, and that if I could do it once, I damn sure could do it again.

Knowing this, the employment of our inherent gifts of grit and willpower from one's stockpile enables people to naturally begin training their minds out of wanting to tap out early. Employing that passion towards achieving your long-term goals transforms your mind, making it a bulldozer to those would-be hurdles. This is not however something that happens, literally or figuratively, overnight. This is the second area where people, me included, often get tripped up.

At the beginning of any personal transformation usually comes the realization of just how much work will go into you accomplishing what you want to, whether it be losing weight, achieving a certain professional standing, or opening lines of communication with once important people in your life. These are just a few examples on a much longer list of why and how people choose to transform their lives.

In my own case, I wanted to regain control of my mind, my body, and most of all, my tattered spirit. I wanted to feel confident and comfortable in my own skin again. That would come, for me, by losing weight.

***

When I learned of David Goggins' 40 Percent Rule, I was already in my fourth year of my journey to bettering my overall health and wellness. Everything that I actively worked on to that point—not needing external validation, losing weight, working out every day, pursuing professional endeavors—were becoming darker and much more difficult. I moved in with my wife, then-girlfriend, into a beautiful apartment complex in Chicago's River North neighborhood.

I spent the year prior grinding as a performer in The Second City's famed Conservatory program in Chicago. As the birthplace of a litany of famous comedians and actors, it provided the next logical step in my journey to professionally performing after moving home from Los Angeles. While I was a growing my professional circle and becoming a successful performer in Los Angeles in both comedic and theatrical respects, I was still an empty shell of a person.

I lived my first month in Los Angeles on the air mattress of a friend of mine who I met through Marquette's improv. group. That first month saw me submit with no abandon to many projects through an online casting database. I auditioned regularly, faced dozens of rejections, and by November, was burnt out. This was not just due to the grind of the entertainment business—I was also in my first ever serious accident that past October. I rear ended a woman's car while driving on the highway at about fifty-five to sixty miles per hour late one night on the way to a film shoot. I had attempted to navigate the crowded and disorienting exits on the famed 101 freeway.

Fortunately, the other driver and I were okay. My car, however, was totaled. I stood on the median of the highway, shaken to my core at the force of the impact all while beginning to feel a deep soreness in my neck from whiplash. I moved to Los Angeles barely two months before, and here I was already in a serious car accident. I called my mom nearly in tears. She talked me through the situation, the police and paramedics arrived at the scene, and being that I was in a place where the only friends I had were around my age, did not know quite who to call for direct, on-the-scene help.

I ended up taking a ride with the tow truck driver, and he dropped me off in the parking lot of a McDonalds where my friend with whom I was living with at the time agreed to pick me up. He sounded urgent on the phone as I talked to him, sheepishly admitting what I had just done. As he picked me up, he was quieter, and we did not say much to each other on the ride back. He would later "tease" me about how shaken up I seemed when he picked me up. He had no idea that I was having regular nightmares not only about the crash but also about what my future would look like in Los Angeles.

I ended up leasing a Honda Civic, and spending eight hours at the dealership to do so after a morning hour-long job interview. I progressively became more and more burnt out as I participated in straight "acting" projects and was confronted with horrifically mean and bullying industry professionals masquerading as tough lovers.

Not ready to give up just yet, I enrolled in an improv. course at the famed Upright Citizens' Brigade (UCB) theater. With the first class, I found a new fire to continue performing.

Improv. comedy, and especially the goofy ensemble-based style of UCB, would regularly leave me fulfilled. Their Improv. 101 class became the forum for my release of energy. I had a successful run-through class and our graduation show. My teacher advised me to try The Groundlings, another famed improv. and sketch comedy theater in LA. Within a week, I was enrolled in an audition to enter their core track of training. I passed my audition, and two weeks later, I walked into Basic Improv. at The Groundlings.

Will Ferrell, Melissa McCarthy, and Kristen Wiig are a couple of the famous alumni who The Groundlings make sure to market. I grew up as a massive Will Ferrell fan, and my own style was often compared to his throughout my career in comedy.

While being in the training center across from the famed Groundlings theater on Melrose Avenue in west Los Angeles was incredible and humbling all at once, the experience was taxing. Class would meet twice a week on Tuesdays and Thursdays from six to ten p.m. I worked a nine-to-five job writing for a company in Santa Monica, which was at least a thirty- to forty-five minute drive to the theater in rush hour traffic in Los Angeles.

Thus, my days would begin around six a.m., when I would wake up, shower, drive the hour west to Santa Monica, leave work, eat dinner on the way to class, and arrive at class around 5:50 p.m., where I would also have to pay for parking on Melrose. This happened twice a week for ten straight weeks.

It was hellish and was made even more so that, as time went on, the grind of Los Angeles living began to expose my true feelings towards the city and the performing profession. In times of adversity, we discover the nuggets of truth that lie well beneath the surface.

In this case, I was living unhappily in a location that felt like a foreign country. Still barely two years into my journey of bettering my overall health and wellness, I was nowhere near where I wanted to be health and happiness-wise. The saving grace was my roommate at the time, Andrew. We met when he was a Marquette senior and I was a sophomore. He was the president of the Fugees improv. group during the year that I joined. We grew close while we were students at Marquette, stayed in regular touch, and found ourselves living together after he moved out west a mere two months after I did. We decided to take the improv. class together, and my life turned around at Christmas time only to find more nosedives down the line.

All this was happening as I was attempting to continue losing weight. By this point, I had probably lost between thirty to forty pounds since graduating Marquette two years prior. For the first ten months of my twelve total living in Los Angeles, I did not belong to a gym. Instead, all I had was a purple resistance band, running shoes, and my workout clothes.

My apartment complex contained a parking lot in the very back. It stretched a full fifty to sixty yards long, with about twenty-five yards of width. It was lit by lampposts at night. Oftentimes, after work, it became my football field. I ran sprints religiously out there—all out down and back. I would jog around our neighborhood and run the beautiful desert hills leading up to steeper mountains surrounding our apartment. If I found myself idle during the day, I would go to the bathroom at work and knock out fifty to one hundred squats and push-ups at a time as well as on every break. Before bed, I was sure to do a few dozen of each again.

This was the part of my journey I was proudest of, though nobody knew about it because of my lack of courage to say so. I was accomplishing an intensely personal goal to lose weight and better my health with very little help from the sources that many people tell us we *need* to achieve this. There were no free weights, treadmills, or air-conditioned gyms for me to employ. I ended up joining one during the summer once I felt I was ready—and even then, I stayed a member for barely two months before finally moving home to Chicago. I did, however, continue my rag-tag workouts on my own while a member.

My year in LA taught me many things, especially as I arrived back home in Chicago, living with my parents as a new graduate of Marquette with no gym membership. I learned how to be resourceful with very little. My workouts at home included runs around my neighborhood before returning home to "lift" in our unfinished basement with my one thirty-pound dumbbell that was nearly ten years old, the same purple resistance band, and miscellaneous benches for dips. It does not sound like much, but it was more than enough. I continued losing weight, and my life changed when I met my now-wife. We began dating that fall, and it was with her that many demons hiding in plain sight within me began to show themselves as she showed me unconditional love and support.

She would mention that certain actions by seeming friends were not normal and were instead flighty or even downright mean. I would often consider this but never possessed the courage to stare that possibility in the face. She changed my life single-handedly in that first year of our dating. I discovered lingering care issues with my long-time doctor, mental health misdiagnoses, and my personal ill fit within the performing industry. I love her with every fiber of my being, and she continues to provide a glowing example to look up to and a force for change in my life every day.

**

This life of working out for hours every week all while learning new eating habits, moving across the country and back, and immersing myself in a variety of professional settings has shown me that whatever excuses we come up with are truly *only* holding us back. I promise you that there were often plenty of days—as there still are—where I did not and do not "feel like" working out or eating properly.

What I also know is that when you have a fire burning inside of you to do or accomplish anything, all it takes is stoking that fire with momentum and *action* to find yourself driven to achieve what you wish to. What it takes is telling yourself, "So DO it."

We can be left feeling inadequate if we don't have the most up-to-date phone, clothes, accessories, etc. This feeling of inadequacy, however, comes directly from an expectation that you have set for yourself, most likely from a source outside of yourself. This won't work, because you will never be or have *exactly* what that source conveys. Instead, we need to find the ability within us to bring that focus to ourselves. Instead, we should ask, "Do I measure up to the standard *I* set for *myself* 'X' number of years ago when I started this journey?" That is a helpful question to ask because it allows you to focus on your own personal progress.

It's wonderful to have people who inspire, motivate, and cultivate drive in you. What we must recognize, however—and what it took me a couple of years to truly understand—is that we are the main protagonists in our stories. We are not living as side characters in someone else's movie no matter how important the world tells you they are. You are the star, writer, director, producer, set designer, costume designer, and main character of *your* movie. When adversity hits, as we've covered, what our favorite characters often do is continue to fight until they achieve the victory that they have long striven towards.

Learning to embrace the grimy, unfinished basement and runs in the sub-zero Chicago weather took me time. Looking back, however, I would not choose to change one thing.

You want to change your life? Okay.

So do it.

Acknowledgments & Final Thoughts

Thank you.

I want to start by saying thank you to those who read this. Your eyes passing over these words mean the world and more to me.

Most of all, I want to thank my wife, Amanda. She has been the source of strength when I have run low at an innumerable amount of points in my journey. Seeing life through her beautifully optimistic perspective has often helped me find reserves when I needed it most. She is my rock, my everything, and I love her with all my being. Thank you, my love.

My family has also seen my metamorphosis. I love you all, and thank you for being the support system within the support system. My parents Steve and Anna, my siblings Nick and Katie, and my in-laws Michael and Diane Trickey and Michele Trickey and Mike Thomas all hold a special place in my heart.

My oldest friend Jon sat through a phone interview for the book. Thank you so much, bud, and your love and support mean the world.

To Andrew, my LA roommate and honorary older brother: thank you for being so steadfast in your care and love.

To Tim Cigelske: thank you for all your time and thoughtfulness during our interview. It made for a rich source of consideration for me during a time when it was needed.

To Professor Koester: thank you for encouraging me to put my story out into the world.

To past professors, teachers, mentors, and coaches who always encouraged me: thank you for seeing what you did in me. It still means the world today.

To all of those who contributed to my Indiegogo Campaign: Tommy Gill, Henry Chong, James Duffy, Deanna DiCristina, Lynne Cohen, Matt Czyl, The Perhats Family, Mary Ellen Keneally, The Kolosky Family, Alex Lee, Sabrina St. Peter, Aunt Colleen & Uncy, Mary DiCristina, Andrea DiCristina, Chris Hoffman, Kent & Alexa Liederbach, Brendan Takash, Matt Greco, Uncle Rob & Aunt Rebecca, Natalie Schuldes, Mason Eddy, Josiah & Rachel Laubenstein, Kyle Synowiec, Gilberto Vaquero, Aunt Cindy & Uncle Joe, Erica De Los Santos-Gerber, Armando & the whole Ronconi family, Mr. and Mrs. Pauly, Casey Hall, Janel Wasisco, Kristina Loy, Jennifer Latimore, George Bicknell, Molly Sroka, Gracie Coletta, Colleen Foy, James Harden, Daniel Christian Luse, Alex Rogalski, Nick Mathis, Miles Hendrick, Clarissa Francis, Jenny

Gassner, Pat Hasselbeck, Cydne Perhats, Carissa Casula Timm, Uncle Mike & Aunt Mary, Andrea Casula, Hannah Fray, Natalie King, Deb Cecsarini, Calvin & Melissa Cohen, Mary Tag, Christie & Larry Shore, Jonathan Robles, Alejandro Argueta, Andrew Gothelf, Jenna Singer, and Rob Ziffra. Your generosity and selflessness during a once-in-a-century global pandemic made this book possible. Thank you from the bottom of my heart.

To past bullies, doubters, and people who wished failure on me: thank you.

***

My purpose in writing this was never to create a cheap self-help book aiming to bring you an instantly gratifying outcome or to glamorize my life or myself. I am far from perfect and genuinely harbor no ill will towards any bullies whom I discussed. This is precisely the point, too: nobody is perfect. That is why I hope that this book can resonate with you no matter your age, race, sex, religion, upbringing, or background.

I am sure that many people who have been through much have been told, "WOW! You should write a book!" Experiences often sound invigorating from the outside looking in, even if for the would-be author they can be truly traumatic to re-live. There certainly was a level of trauma for me in sitting down to re-hash the hardest moments of my life, but I can honestly tell you that all that trauma I experienced in re-living and writing was well worth it—and that is the root of why I *needed* to write.

Personally, I am immensely fortunate with a loving family, a beautiful wife, and the means to live a life that can be comfortable. I am grateful to no end for that fortune; however, how I know I have come to define "fortunate" includes elements that I know with a great deal of certainty others might not include. Those other factors include the continued exposure to physical and emotional pain, seeing the beginnings of the depths of despair, being rejected with frequency, and living with a blanket of depression and anxiety. Confessing my gratefulness for each of these can absolutely sound cheap because it's always easier to speak about discomfort and unease from a place of comfort and that's exactly what I am doing now. I can also tell you with certainty that gratefulness only begins to describe my deep affection for each of those seemingly awful things.

I was not always like this. I grew up with an only flight reflex—there was no "fight" corollary. My natural born instinct was always to stop whatever was making me uncomfortable almost immediately and quit. Here's a true story: I quit karate about ten minutes into the first session when I could not do a push-up. I lived much of the first twenty-five years of my life in fear. I was a shy child whose demeanor changed so much as a young adult that I could not adjust adequately, and so I lost my identity and sense of self.

We often learn more about ourselves at our valleys than we do at our peaks; therefore, I wanted to share my story with you. I have come to believe, through my own life's journey that the bottom is where we learn. Comfort that comes from peaking can be more dangerous for some than a despair-fueled valley—I know because I lived that.

As you move forward, it is important to remember that bullies are some of the most hurt, insecure, and unstable people you could ever hope to cross paths with. Those who actively put others down, talk behind backs, and place others into categories below them are doing so from a place of pain. They often do not acknowledge it, but that is another hallmark of a suffering person: one who lacks the courage and wherewithal to look at and reflect on their flaws plainly and without judgment.

Not everybody chooses to direct their pain outward—for my part, I internalized much of it. While going through a hardship while in college at Marquette, I was outwardly happy-go-lucky. Nothing seemed to bother me, as former classmates have now told me. I seemed utterly unflappable, joyous, and oblivious to any snarkiness, pettiness, and bullying by those surrounding me while at Marquette. Though I may have appeared that way, none of that was true.

Another foundational building block for my own growth has been the realization that, through it all, I am still here. You're reading this, so despite all the suffering, pain, anguish, and deep lows—and in part because of the euphoria and joy you have undoubtedly experienced—so are you.

Mainly, this is not meant to glamorize myself. Some might take it that way, and that's okay. What I have wanted to convey, and what I hope you have taken away is that if I can do it, *so can you*. This is about you, the reader. What I hope is that you have discovered powers you didn't know you had—or those that you did not want to acknowledge but now feel the urge to.

Most importantly and with all this said, my book is by no means a cure-all for mental illness. This was my experience and the lessons I have learned presented with the hope that some of you will find that it applies to you in digging yourself out of a rut. It will not apply to everybody.

Getting help can be the most powerful thing one can do for oneself, so please, if you find yourself feeling majorly depressed, seek help. If you're considering hurting yourself and need to talk to someone now, the national suicide hotline is 1-800-273-8255. Your mental health and well-being are most important.

Love to you all. Keep on going.

References

INTRODUCTION

2019 Global Emotions Report. Washington, DC: Gallup, Inc. Published April 2019. Accessed December 15, 2019. https://www.gallup.com/analytics/248906/gallup-global-emotions-report-2019.aspx.

Goggins, David. *Can't Hurt Me: Master Your Mind and Defy the Odds.* Austin, Texas: Lioncrest Publishing. 2018.

TED. "Grit: The Power of Passion and Perseverance | Angela Lee Duckworth." May 9, 2013. Video, 6:12. https://www.youtube.com/watch?v=H14bBuluwB8.

TED. "How to Make Stress Your Friend | Kelly McGonigal." September 4, 2013. Video, 14:28. https://www.youtube.com/watch?v=RcGyVTAoXEU&vl=en.

CHAPTER 1

"8 Reasons It Wasn't Easy Being Spartan." History Channel Online, Evan Andrews. Accessed January 3, 2019. https://www.history.com/news/8-reasons-it-wasnt-easy-being-spartan.

Agamemnon. Translated in verse by Robin Bond. Christchurch, New Zealand: University of Canterbury, 2014.

Constable, Giles. *Attitudes toward self-inflicted suffering in the Middle Ages.* Brookline, Mass: Hellenic College Press, 1982.

Liebert, Hugh. *Plutarch's Politics: Between City and Empire.* New York: Cambridge University Press, 2016.

Nietzsche, Friedrich. *The Birth of Tragedy.* Translated by William A. Haussmann. Boston: Digireads.com Publishing, 2018.

Nietzsche, Friedrich. *The Gay Science.* Translated by Thomas Common. Edinburgh: The Darien Press, 1910. Accessed via The Gutenberg Project e-Library. https://www.gutenberg.org/files/52881/52881-h/52881-h.htm.

Snyder, Zach, dir. *300.* 2007; Burbank, CA: Warner Bros. Pictures, 2013. Blu-ray Disc, 1080p HD.

Spartan Race. "What is Spartan?" The Origin of Spartan. Accessed January 5, 2019. https://race.spartan.com/en/what-is-spartan.

Steiner, Rudolf. "The Origin of Suffering." Lecture. Berlin. November 8, 1906. Transcript. The Rudolf Steiner Internet Archive and e.Lib. https://wn.rsarchive.org/Lectures/GA055/English/SBC1980/19061108p01.html.

Suskin, Jeff. *The Ooda: The Lifestyle of Awareness* (blog). *Medium*, January 1, 2014. https://medium.com/the-ooda/the-etymology-of-suffering-1d330ddfd94a.

CHAPTER 2

Balestrieri, Steve. "Remembering Navy SEAL Michael P. Murphy, Medal of Honor 6/28/2005." *SOFREP*, June 29, 2017. https://sofrep.com/specialoperations/remembering-navy-seal-michael-p-murphy-medal-honor/.

Brittanica. "Newton's laws of motion." Science. Accessed January 12, 2020. https://www.britannica.com/science/Newtons-laws-of-motion.

Goalcast. "How to Conquer Your Mind and Embrace The Suck | David Goggins." November 11, 2017. Video, 10:31. https://www.youtube.com/watch?v=_J_bOqPhuZA.

Goggins, David. *Can't Hurt Me: Master Your Mind and Defy the Odds.* Austin, Texas: Lioncrest Publishing. 2018.

Merriam-Webster. s.v. "governor (n.)." Accessed January 2, 2020. https://www.merriam-webster.com/dictionary/governor.

Muhammad Ali. "I hated every minute of training, but I said, 'Don't quit. Suffer now and live the rest of your life as a champion.'" Twitter, October 15, 2012. https://twitter.com/MuhammadAli/status/864155925925552128.

Special Operations Warrior Foundation. "Mission, Vision and Values." Who We Are. Accessed January 11, 2020. https://specialops.org/our-mission/.

CHAPTER 3

Altieri, Kevin, dir. *Batman: The Animated Series*. Episode 1, "The Cat and the Claw Part I." Written by Jules Dennis and Richard Mueller. Featuring Kevin Conroy. Aired September 5, 1992, on Fox Kids.

Goggins, David. *Can't Hurt Me: Master Your Mind and Defy the Odds.* Austin, Texas: Lioncrest Publishing. 2018.

Lasseter, John, dir. *Toy Story.* 1997; Emeryville, CA: Walt Disney-Pixar Animation, 2019. Blu-ray Disc, 1080p HD.

Nolan, Christopher, dir. *Batman Begins.* 2005; Burbank, CA: Warner Bros. Pictures, 2008. Blu-ray Disc, 1080p HD.

Staskiewicz, Keith. "Ben Affleck: 'Batman is basically the American version of Hamlet'." Entertainment Weekly, July 1, 2015. Accessed January 3, 2020. https://ew.com/comic-con/2015/07/01/ben-affleck-batman-hamlet/.

Variety. "Robert Pattinson Talks 'The Batman'." September 3, 2019. Video, 5:30. https://www.youtube.com/watch?v=TaoJm-1RRKE0.

CHAPTER 4

Tom Bilyeu. "Become A Savage & Live On Your Own Terms | David Goggins on Impact Theory." December 11, 2018. Video, 53:41. https://www.youtube.com/watch?v=dIM7E8e9JKY.

CHAPTER 5

Farley, Tom Jr. and Tanner Colby. *The Chris Farley Show: A Biography in Three Acts.* New York: Penguin Group USA, 2008.

Goggins, David. *Can't Hurt Me: Master Your Mind and Defy the Odds.* Austin, Texas: Lioncrest Publishing. 2018.

Patton, George S. *Military Essays and Articles*, edited by Charles M. Province, 65. San Diego, California: The George S. Patton Jr. Historical Society, 2002. http://www.pattonhq.com/pdffiles/vintagetext.pdf.

CHAPTER 6

2019 Global Emotions Report. Washington, DC: Gallup, Inc. Published April 2019. Accessed December 15, 2019. https://www.gallup.com/analytics/248906/gallup-global-emotions-report-2019.aspx.

Jefferson, Thomas, et al. *The Declaration of Independence.* July 4, 1776. Manuscript/mixed material. The Thomas Jefferson Papers at the Library of Congress. https://www.loc.gov/item/mtjbib000159/.

Raypole, Crystal and Dr. Timothy J. Legg. "How to Hack Your Hormones for a Better Mood." Healthline. Accessed January 2, 2020. https://www.healthline.com/health/happy-hormone.

NBC News. "Octavia Spencer's Kent State Speech 2017 Commencement (Full)." May 31, 2017. Video, 23:47. https://www.youtube.com/watch?v=0KW_dH_919w.

CHAPTER 7

Marlowe, Christopher. *The London Series of English Classics: Doctor Faustus.* Notations by Wilhelm Wagner. London, England: Longmans, Green, and Co., 1918.

Snyder, Zach, dir. *Man of Steel.* 2013; Burbank, CA: Warner Bros. Pictures, 2013. Blu-ray Disc, 1080p HD.

CHAPTER 8

Berman, Mark G., Ethan Kross, Katherine M Krpan, Mary K Askren, Aleah Burson, Patricia J Deldin, Stephen Kaplan, Lindsey Sherdell, Ian H Gotlib, John Jonides. "Interacting with nature improves cognition and affect for individuals with depression." *Journal of Affective Disorders* 140, issue 3 (November 2012): 300-305. https://www.sciencedirect.com/science/article/abs/pii/S0165032712002005?via%3Dihub.

Edelhauser, Kristin. "John Wooden's Pyramid Still Standing." Entrepreneur. Accessed January 3, 2020. https://www.entrepreneur.com/article/176282.

Merriam-Webster. s.v. "hypertrophy (n.)." Accessed January 2, 2020. https://www.merriam-webster.com/dictionary/hypertrophy.

National Institute of Neurological Disorders and Stroke. "Brain Basics: Understanding Sleep." Patient & Caregiver Information. Accessed January 2, 2020. https://www.ninds.nih.gov/Disorders/Patient-Caregiver-Education/Understanding-Sleep.

Rabbitt, Meghan. "11 Biggest Benefits of Walking to Improve Your Health, According to Doctors." Prevention. Accessed January 5, 2020. https://www.prevention.com/fitness/a20485587/benefits-from-walking-every-day/.

National Institute of Neurological Disorders and Stroke. "Brain Basics: Understanding Sleep." Patient & Caregiver Information. Accessed January 2, 2020. https://www.ninds.nih.gov/Disorders/Patient-Caregiver-Education/Understanding-Sleep.

The Wooden Effect. "About the Pyramid of Success." About Coach. Accessed January 3, 2020. https://www.thewoodeneffect.com/pyramid-of-success/

CHAPTER 9

Barton Perry, Ralph. *The Thought and Character of William James.* Nashville, TN: Vanderbilt University Press, 1996.

James, William. *Pragmatism and Other Writings.* New York: Penguin Classics, 2000. Kindle.

James, William. *Principles of Psychology, Vol. 2., Revised Ed.* Garden City, New York: Dover Publications, 2012. Kindle.

James, William. *The Varieties of Religious Experience: A Study in Human Nature.* London: Longmans, Green, and Co., 1851. eBook. http://www.gutenberg.org/files/621/621-h/621-h.html.

Merriam-Webster. s.v. "vulnerable (n.)." Accessed February 12, 2021. https://www.merriam-webster.com/dictionary/vulnerable.

CHAPTER 10

DavidGoggins.com. "There is Only One David Goggins." About. Accessed January 12, 2020.

DavidGoggins.com. "Years of Athletic Achievement." Achievements. Accessed January 12, 2020.

Goggins, David. *Can't Hurt Me: Master Your Mind and Defy the Odds.* Austin, Texas: Lioncrest Publishing. 2018.

Merriam-Webster. s.v. "impostor syndrome (n.)." Accessed January 10, 2020. https://www.merriam-webster.com/dictionary/impostor%20syndrome.

StopBullying.gov. "Effects of Bullying." Bullying. Last modified July 21, 2020. https://www.stopbullying.gov/bullying/effects.

StopBullying.gov. "Facts About Bullying." Resources. Last modified August 12, 2020. https://www.stopbullying.gov/resources/facts#stats.

TED. "Grit: the power of passion and perseverance | Angela Lee Duckworth." May 9, 2013. Video, 6:12. https://www.youtube.com/watch/H14bBuluwB8

www.ingramcontent.com/pod-product-compliance
Lightning Source LLC
LaVergne TN
LVHW011829060526
838200LV00053B/3951